Inspired Talks

by

Swami Vivekananda

Inspired Talks
by Swami Vivekananda

ISBN: 978-93-59393-67-4

Published by

DOUBLE 9 BOOKS

2/13-B, Ansari Road
Daryaganj, New Delhi – 110002
info@double9books.com
www.double9books.com
Tel. 011-40042856

This book is under public domain

ABOUT THE AUTHOR

Swami Vivekananda was born Narendranath Datta in India on January 12, 1863. He died on July 4, 1902, and was the most important student of the Indian saint Ramakrishna. He was an important part of bringing Vedanta and Yoga to the West. He is also charged with making people more aware of other religions and making Hinduism a major world religion. Vivekananda had a lot of success at the Parliament. In the years that followed, he gave hundreds of lectures across the United States, England, and Europe to spread the main ideas of Hinduism. He also started the Vedanta Society of New York and the Vedanta Society of San Francisco, which is now the Vedanta Society of Northern California. Both of these groups became the basis for Vedanta Societies in the West. Vivekananda was one of the most important philosophers and social reformers in India at the time. He was also one of the most successful and powerful Vedanta missionaries in the West.People now think of him as one of the most important people in modern India and Hinduism. Mahatma Gandhi said that after reading Vivekananda's works, he loved his country a thousand times more.

CONTENTS

Wednesday, June 19, 1895.

(RECORDED BY MISS S. E. WALDO, A DISCIPLE)

(This day marks the beginning of the regular teaching given daily by Swami Vivekananda to his disciples at Thousand Island Park. We had not yet all assembled there, but the Master's heart was always in his work, so he commenced at once to teach the three or four who were with him. He came on this first morning with the Bible in his hand and opened to the Book of John, saying that since we were all Christians, it was proper that he should begin with the Christian scriptures.)

"In the beginning was the Word, and the Word was with God, and the Word was God." The Hindu calls this Mâyâ, the manifestation of God, because it is the power of God. The Absolute reflecting through the universe is what we call nature. The Word has two manifestations — the general one of nature, and the special one of the great Incarnations of God — Krishna, Buddha, Jesus, and Ramakrishna. Christ, the special manifestation of the Absolute, is known and knowable. The absolute cannot be known: we cannot know the Father, only the Son. We can only see the Absolute through the "tint of humanity", through Christ.

In the first five verses of John is the whole essence of Christianity: each verse is full of the profoundest philosophy.

The Perfect never becomes imperfect. It is in the darkness, but is not affected by the darkness. God's mercy goes to all, but is not affected by their wickedness. The sun is not affected by any disease of our eyes which may make us see it distorted. In the twenty-ninth verse, "taketh away the sin of the world" means that Christ would show us the way to become perfect. God became Christ to show man his true nature, that we too are God. We are human coverings over the Divine; but as the divine Man, Christ and we are one.

The Trinitarian Christ is elevated above us; the Unitarian Christ is merely a moral man; neither can help us. The Christ who is the Incarnation of God, who has not forgotten His divinity, that Christ can help us, in Him there is no imperfection. These Incarnations are always conscious of their own divinity; they know it from their birth. They are like the actors whose play is over, but who, after their work is done, return to please others. These great Ones are untouched by aught of earth; they assume our form and our limitations for a time in order to teach us; but in reality they are never limited, they are ever free. . . .

Good is near Truth, but is not yet Truth. After learning not to be disturbed by evil, we have to learn not to be made happy by good. We must find that we are beyond both evil and good; we must study their adjustment and see that they are both necessary.

The idea of dualism is from the ancient Persians. Really good and evil are one (Because they are both chains and products of Maya.) and are in our own mind. When the mind is self-poised, neither good nor bad affects it. Be perfectly free; then neither can affect it, and we enjoy freedom and bliss. Evil is the iron chain, good is the gold one; both are chains. Be free, and know once for all that there is no chain for you. Lay hold of the golden chain to loosen the hold of the iron one, then throw both away. The thorn of evil is in our flesh; take another thorn from the same bush and extract the first thorn; then throw away both and be free. . . .

In the world take always the position of the giver. Give everything and look for no return. Give love, give help, give service, give any little thing you can, but *keep out barter*. Make no conditions, and none will be imposed. Let us give out of our own bounty, just as God gives to us.

The Lord is the only Giver, all the men in the world are only shopkeepers. Get His cheque, and it must be honoured everywhere.

"God is the inexplicable, inexpressible essence of love", to be known, but never defined.

* * *

In our miseries and struggles the world seems to us a very dreadful place. But just as when we watch two puppies playing and biting we do not concern ourselves at all, realising that it is only fun and that even a sharp nip now and then will do no actual harm, so all our struggles are but play in God's eyes. This world is all for play and only amuses God; nothing in it can make God angry.

* * *

"Mother! In the sea of life my bark is sinking.

The whirlwind of illusion, the storm of attachment is growing every moment.

My five oarsmen (senses) are foolish, and the helmsman (mind) is weak.

My bearings are lost, my boat is sinking.

O Mother! Save me!"

"Mother, Thy light stops not for the saint or the sinner; it animates the lover and the murderer." Mother is ever manifesting through all. The light is not polluted by what it shines on, nor benefited by it. The light is ever pure, ever changeless. Behind every creature is the "Mother", pure, lovely, never changing. "Mother, manifested as light in all beings, we bow down to Thee!" She is equally in suffering, hunger, pleasure, sublimity. "When the bee sucks honey, the Lord is eating." Knowing that the Lord is everywhere, the sages give up praising and blaming. *Know* that nothing can hurt you. How? Are you not free? Are you not Âtman? He is the Life of our lives, the hearing of our ears, the sight of our eyes.

We go through the world like a man pursued by a policeman and see the barest glimpses of the beauty of it. All this fear that pursues us comes from believing in matter. Matter gets its whole existence from the presence of mind behind it. What we see is God percolating through nature. (Here "nature" means matter and mind.)

Sunday, June 23, 1895.

(RECORDED BY MISS S. E. WALDO, A DISCIPLE)

Be brave and be sincere; then follow any path with devotion, and you *must* reach the Whole. Once lay hold of one link of the chain, and the whole chain must come by degrees. Water the roots of the tree (that is, reach the Lord), and the whole tree is watered; getting the Lord, we get all.

One-sidedness is the bane of the world. The more sides you can develop the more souls you have, and you can see the universe through all souls — through the Bhakta (devotee) and the Jnâni (philosopher). Determine your own nature and stick to it. Nishthâ (devotion to one ideal) is the only method for the beginner; but with devotion and sincerity it will lead to all. Churches, doctrines, forms, are the hedges to protect the tender plant, but they must later be broken down that the plant may become a tree. So the various religions, Bibles, Vedas, dogmas — all are just tubs for the little plant; but it must get out of the tub. Nishthâ is, in a manner, placing the plant in the tub, shielding the struggling soul in its path. . . .

Look at the "ocean" and not at the "wave"; see no difference between ant and angel. Every worm is the brother of the Nazarene. How say one is greater and one less? Each is great in his own place. We are in the sun and in the stars as much as here. Spirit is beyond space and time and is everywhere. Every mouth praising the Lord is my mouth, every eye seeing is my eye. We are confined nowhere; we are not body, the universe is our body. We are magicians waving magic wands and creating scenes before us at will. We are the spider in his huge web, who can go on the varied strands wheresoever he desires. The spider is now only conscious of the spot where he is, but he will in time become conscious of the whole web. We are now conscious only where the body is, we can use only one brain; but when we reach ultraconsciousness, we know all, we can use all brains. Even now we can "give the push" in consciousness, and it goes beyond and acts in the superconscious.

We are striving "to be" and nothing more, no "I" ever — just pure crystal, reflecting all, but ever the same, When that state is reached, there is no more doing; the body becomes a mere mechanism, pure without care for it; it cannot become impure.

Know you are the Infinite, then fear must die. Say ever, "I and my Father are one."

* * *

In time to come Christs will be in numbers like bunches of grapes on a vine; then the play will be over and will pass out — as water in a kettle beginning to boil shows first one bubble, then another then more and more, until all is in ebullition and passes out as steam. Buddha and Christ are the two biggest "bubbles" the world has yet produced. Moses was a tiny bubble, greater and greater ones came. Sometime, however, all will be bubbles and escape; but creation, ever new, will bring new water to go through the process all over again.

Monday, June 24, 1895.

(REcorded By MIss S. E. WAldo, A Disciple)

(*The reading today was from the Bhakti-Sutras by Nârada.*)

"Extreme love to God is Bhakti, and this love is the real immortality, getting which a man becomes perfectly satisfied, sorrows for no loss, and is never jealous; knowing which man becomes mad."

My Master used to say, "This world is a huge lunatic asylum where all men are mad, some after money, some after women, some after name or fame, and a few after God. I prefer to be mad after God. God is the philosophers' stone that turns us to gold in an instant; the form remains, but the nature is changed — the human form remains, but no more can we hurt or sin."

"Thinking of God, some weep, some sing, some laugh, some dance, some say wonderful things, but all speak of nothing but God."

Prophets preach, but the Incarnations like Jesus, Buddha, Ramakrishna, can give religion; one glance, one touch is enough. That is the power of the Holy Ghost, the "laying on of hands"; the power was actually transmitted to the disciples by the Master — the "chain of Guru-power". That, the real baptism, has been handed down for untold ages.

"Bhakti cannot be used to fulfil any desires, itself being the check to all desires." Narada gives these as the signs of love: "When all thoughts, all words, and all deeds are given up unto the Lord, and the least forgetfulness of God makes one intensely miserable, then love has begun."

"This is the highest form of love because therein is no desire for reciprocity, which desire is in all human love."

"A man who has gone beyond social and scriptural usage, he is a Sannyâsin. When the whole soul goes to God, when we take refuge only in God, then we know that we are about to get this love."

Obey the scriptures until you are strong enough to do without them; then go beyond them. Books are not an end-all. Verification is the only proof of religious truth. Each must verify for himself; and no teacher who says, "I have seen, but *you* cannot", is to be trusted, only that one who says, "You can see too". All scriptures, all truths are Vedas in all times, in all countries; because these truths are to be *seen*, and any one may discover them.

"When the sun of Love begins to break on the horizon, we want to give up all our actions unto God; and when we forget Him for a moment, it grieves us greatly."

Let nothing stand between God and your love for Him. Love Him, love Him, love Him; and let the world say what it will. Love is of three sorts — one demands, but gives nothing; the second is exchange; and the third is love without thought of return — love like that of the moth for the light.

"Love is higher than work, than Yoga, than knowledge."

Work is merely a schooling for the doer; it can do no good to others. We must work out our own problem; the prophets only show us how to work. *"What you think, you become"*, so if you throw your burden on Jesus, you will have to think of Him and thus become like Him — you *love* Him.

"Extreme love and highest knowledge are one."

But theorising about God will not do; we must love and work. Give up the world and all worldly things, especially while the "plant" is tender. Day and night think of God and think of nothing else as far as possible. The daily necessary thoughts can all be thought through God. Eat to Him, drink to Him, sleep to Him, see Him in all. Talk of God to others; this is most beneficial.

Get the mercy of God and of His greatest children: these are the two chief ways to God. The company of these children of light is very hard to get; five minutes in their company will change a whole life; and if you really want it enough, one will come to you. The presence of those who love God makes a place holy, "such is the glory of the children of the Lord". They are He; and when they speak, their words are scriptures. The place where they have been becomes filled with their vibrations, and those going there feel them and have a tendency to become holy also.

"To such lovers there is no distinction of caste, learning, beauty, birth, wealth, or occupation; because all are His."

Give up all evil company, especially at the beginning. Avoid worldly company, that will distract your mind. *Give up all "me and mine"*. To him who has nothing in the universe the Lord comes. Cut the bondage of all worldly affections; go beyond laziness and all care as to what becomes of you. Never turn back to see the result of what you have done. Give all to the Lord and go on and think not of it. The whole soul pours in a continuous current to God; there is no time to seek money, or name, or fame, no time to think of anything but God; then will come into our hearts that infinite, wonderful bliss of Love. All desires are but beads of glass. Love of God increases every moment and is ever new, to be known only by feeling it. Love is the easiest of all, it waits for no logic, it is natural. We need no demonstration, no proof. Reasoning is limiting something by our own minds. We throw a net and catch something, and then say that we have demonstrated it; but never, never can we catch God in a net.

Love should be unrelated. Even when we love wrongly, it is of the true love, of the true bliss; the power is the same, use it as we may. Its very nature is peace and bliss. The murderer when he kisses his baby forgets for an instant all but love. Give up all self, all egotism s get out of anger, lust, give *all* to God. "I am not, but Thou art; the old man is all gone, only Thou remainest." "I am Thou." Blame none; if evil comes, know the Lord is playing with you and be exceeding glad.

Love is beyond time and space, it is absolute.

Tuesday, June 25, 1895.

After every happiness comes misery; they may be far apart or near. The more advanced the soul, the more quickly does one follow the other. *What we want is neither happiness nor misery.* Both make us forget our true nature; both are chains — one iron, one gold; behind both is the Atman, who knows neither happiness nor misery. These are *states* and states must ever change; but the nature of the Soul is bliss, peace, unchanging. We have not to get it, we have it; only wash away the dross and see it.

Stand upon the Self, then only can we truly love the world. Take a very, very high stand; knowing out universal nature, we must look with perfect calmness upon all the *panorama* of the world. It is but baby's play, and we know that, so cannot be disturbed by it. If the mind is pleased with praise, it will be displeased with blame. All pleasures of the senses or even of the mind are evanescent but within ourselves is the one true unrelated pleasure, dependent upon nothing. It is perfectly free, it is bliss. *The more our bliss is within, the more spiritual we are.* The pleasure of the Self is what the world calls religion.

The internal universe, the *real*, is infinitely greater than the external, which is only a shadowy projection of the true one. This world is neither true nor untrue, it is the shadow of truth. "Imagination is the gilded shadow of truth", says the poet.

We enter into creation, and then for us it becomes living. Things are dead in themselves; only we give them life, and then, like fools, we turn around and are afraid of them, or enjoy them. But be not like certain fisher-women, who, caught in a storm on their way home from market, took refuge in the house of a florist. They were lodged for the night in a room next to the garden where the air was full of the fragrance of flowers. In vain did they try to rest, until one of their number suggested that they wet their fishy baskets and place them near their heads. Then they all fell into a sound sleep.

The world is our fish basket, we must not depend upon it for enjoyment. Those who do are the Tâmasas or the bound. Then there are the Râjasas or the egotistical, who talk always about "I", "I". They do good work sometimes and may become spiritual. But the highest are the Sâttvikas, the introspective, those who live only in the Self. These three qualities, Tamas, Rajas, and Sattva (idleness, activity, and illumination), are in everyone, and different ones predominate at different times.

Creation is not a "making" of something, it is the struggle to regain the equilibrium, as when atoms of cork are thrown to the bottom of a pail of water and rush to rise to the top, singly or in clusters. *Life is and must be accompanied by evil.* A little evil is the source of life; the little wickedness that is in the world is very good; for when the balance is regained, the world will end, because sameness and destruction are one. When this world goes, good and evil go with it; but when we can transcend this world, we get rid of both good and evil and have bliss.

There is no possibility of ever having pleasure without pain, good without evil; for living itself is just the lost equilibrium. What we want is freedom, not life, nor pleasure, nor good. Creation is infinite, without beginning and without end — the ever-moving ripple in an infinite lake. There are yet unreached depths and others where the equilibrium has been regained; but the ripple is always progressing, the struggle to regain the balance is eternal. Life and death are only different names for the same fact, the two sides of the one coin. Both are Maya, the inexplicable state of striving at one time to live, and a moment later to die. Beyond this is the true nature, the Atman. While we recognise a God, it is really only the Self which we have separated ourselves from and worship as outside of us; but it is our true Self all the time — the one and only God.

To regain the balance we must counteract Tamas by Rajas; then conquer Rajas by Sattva, the calm beautiful state that will grow and grow until all else is gone. Give up bondage; become a son, be free, and then you can "see the Father", as did Jesus. Infinite strength is religion and God. Avoid weakness and slavery. You are only a soul, *if* you are free; there is immortality for you, *if* you are free; there is God, *if* He is free. . . .

The world for me, not I for the world. Good and evil are our slaves, not we theirs. It is the nature of the brute to remain where he is (not to progress); it is the nature of man to seek good and avoid evil; it is the nature of God to seek neither, but just to be eternally blissful. Let us be God! Make the heart like an ocean, go beyond all the trifles of the world, be mad with joy even at evil; see the world as a picture and then enjoy its beauty, knowing that nothing affects you. Children finding glass beads in a mud puddle, that is the good of the world. Look at it with calm complacency; see good and evil as the same — both are merely "God's play"; enjoy all.

* * *

My Master used to say, "All is God; but tiger-God is to be shunned. All water is water; but we avoid dirty water for drinking."

The whole sky is the censer of God, and sun and moon are the lamps. What temple is needed? All eyes are Thine, yet Thou hast not an eye; all hands are Thine; yet Thou hast not a hand.

Neither seek nor avoid, take what comes. It is liberty to be affected by nothing; do not merely endure, be unattached. Remember the story of the bull. A mosquito sat long on the horn of a certain bull. Then his conscience troubled him, and he said, "Mr. Bull, I have been sitting here a long time, perhaps I annoy you. I am sorry, I will go away." But the bull replied, "Oh no, not at all! Bring your whole family and live on my horn; what can you do to me?"

Wednesday, June 26, 1895.

Our best work is done, our greatest influence is exerted, when we are without thought of self. All great geniuses know this. Let us open ourselves to the one Divine Actor, and let Him act, and do nothing ourselves. "*O Arjuna! I have no duty in the whole world*", says Krishna. Be perfectly resigned, perfectly unconcerned; then alone can you do any true work. No eyes can see the real forces, we can only see the results. Put out self, lose it, forget it; just let God work, it is His business. We have nothing to do but stand aside and let God work. The more we go away, the more God comes in. Get rid of the little "I", and let only the great "I" live.

We are what our thoughts have made us; so take care of what you think. Words are secondary. Thoughts live, they travel far. Each thought we think is tinged with our own character, so that for the pure and holy man, even his jests or abuse will have the twist of his own love and purity and do good.

Desire nothing; think of God and look for no return. It is the desireless who bring results. The begging monks carry religion to every man's door; but they think that they do nothing, they claim nothing, their work is unconsciously done. If they should eat of the tree of knowledge, they would become egoists, and all the good they do would fly away. As soon as we say "I", we are humbugged all the time; and we call it "knowable", but it is only going round and round like a bullock tied to a tree. The Lord has hidden Himself best, and His work is best; so he who hides himself best, accomplishes most. Conquer *yourself*, and the whole universe is yours.

In the state of Sattva we see the very nature of things, we go beyond the senses and beyond reason. The adamantine wall that shuts us in is egoism; we refer everything to ourselves, thinking. "I do this, that, and the other." Get rid of this puny "I"; kill this diabolism in us; "Not I, but Thou" — say it, feel it, live it. Until we give up the world manufactured by the ego, never can we enter the kingdom of heaven. None ever did, none ever will. To give up the world is to forget the ego, to know it not at all — living *in* the body, but not *of* it. This rascal ego must be obliterated. Bless men when they revile you. Think how much good they are doing you; they can only hurt themselves. Go where people hate you, let them thrash the ego out of you, and you will get nearer to the Lord. Like the mother-monkey, we hug our "baby", the world, as long as we can, but at last when we are driven to put it under our feet and step on it then we are ready to come to God. Blessed it is to be persecuted for the sake of righteousness. Blessed are we if we cannot read, we have less to take us away from God.

Enjoyment is the million-headed serpent that we must tread under foot. We renounce and go on, then find nothing and despair; but hold on, *hold on*. The world is a demon. It is a kingdom of which the puny ego is king. Put it away and stand firm. Give up lust and gold and fame and hold fast to the Lord, and at last we shall reach a state of perfect indifference. The idea that the gratification of the senses constitutes enjoyment is purely materialistic. There is not one spark of real enjoyment there; all the joy there is, is a mere reflection of the true bliss.

Those who give themselves up to the Lord do more for the world than all the so-called workers. One man who has purified himself thoroughly accomplishes more than a regiment of preachers. *Out of purity and silence comes the word of power.*

"Be like a lily — stay in one place and expand your petals; and the bees will come of themselves." There was a great contrast between Keshab Chandra Sen and Shri Ramakrishna. The second never recognised any sin or misery in the world, no evil to fight against. The first was a great ethical reformer, leader, and founder of the Brahmo-Samaj. After twelve years the quiet prophet of Dakshineswar had worked a revolution not only in India, but in the world. The power is with the silent ones, who only live and love and then withdraw their personality. They never say "me" and "mine"; they are only blessed in being instruments. Such men are the makers of Christs and Buddhas, ever living fully identified with God, ideal existences, asking nothing, and not consciously doing anything. They are the real movers, the Jivanmuktas, (Literally, free even while living.) absolutely selfless, the little personality entirely blown away, ambition non-existent. They are all principle, no personality.

Thursday, June 27, 1895.

(RECORDED BY MISS S. E. WALDO, A DISCIPLE)

*(The Swami brought the New Testament this
morning and talked again on the book of John.)*

Mohammed claimed to be the "Comforter" that Christ promised to send. He considered it unnecessary to claim a supernatural birth for Jesus. Such claims have been common in all ages and in all countries. All great men have claimed gods for their fathers.

Knowing is only relative; we can be God, but never *know* Him. Knowledge is a lower state; Adam's fall was when he came to "know". Before that he was God, he was truth, he was purity. We are our own faces, but can see only a reflection, never the real thing. We are love, but when we think of it, we have to use a phantasm, which proves that matter is only externalised thought.

Nivritti is turning aside from the world. Hindu mythology says that the four first-created (The four first-created were Sanaka, Sanandana, Sanâtana, and Sanatkumâra.) were warned by a Swan (God Himself) that manifestation was only secondary; so they remained without creating. The meaning of this is that expression is degeneration, because Spirit can only be expressed by the letter and then the "letter killeth" (Bible, 2 Cor. III. 6.); yet principle is bound to be clothed in matter, though we know that later we shall lose sight of the real in the covering. Every great teacher understands this, and that is why a continual succession of prophets has to come to show us the principle and give it a new covering suited to the times. My Master taught that religion is one; all prophets teach the same; but they can only present the principle in a form; so they take it out of the old form and put it before us in a new one. When we free ourselves from name and form, especially from a body — when we need no body, good or bad — then only do we escape from bondage. Eternal progression is eternal bondage; annihilation of form is to be preferred. We must get free from any body, even a "god-body". God is the only real existence, there cannot be two. There is but One Soul, and I am That.

Good works are only valuable as a means of escape; they do good to the doer, never to any other.

Knowledge is mere classification. When we find many things of the same kind we call the sum of them by a certain name and are satisfied; we discover "facts", never "why". We take a circuit in a wider field of darkness and think we know something! No "why" can be answered in this world; for that we must go to God. The Knower can never be expressed; it is as when a grain of salt drops into the ocean, it is at once merged in the ocean.

Differentiation creates; homogeneity or sameness is God. Get beyond differentiation; then you conquer life and death and reach eternal sameness and are in God, are God. Get freedom, even at the cost of life. All lives belong to us as leaves to a book; but we are unchanged, the Witness, the Soul, upon whom the impression is made, as when the impression of a circle is made upon the eyes when a firebrand is rapidly whirled round and round. The Soul is the unity of all personalities, and because It is at rest, eternal, unchangeable. It is God, Atman. It is not life, but It is coined into life. It is not pleasure, but It is manufactured into pleasure. . . .

Today God is being abandoned by the world because He does not seem to be doing enough for the world. So they say, "Of what good is He?" Shall we look upon God as a mere municipal authority?

All we can do is to put down all desires, hates, differences; put down the lower self, commit mental suicide, as it were; keep the body and mind pure and healthy, but only as instruments to help us to God; that is their only true use. Seek truth for truth's sake alone, look not for bliss. It may come, but do not let that be your incentives. Have no motive except God. Dare to come to Truth even through hell.

Friday, June 28, 1895.

(RECORDED BY MISS S. E. WALDO, A DISCIPLE)

(The entire party went on a picnic for the day, and although the Swami taught constantly, as he did wherever he was, no notes were taken and no record, therefore, of what he said remains. As he began his breakfast before setting out, however, he remarked:)

Be thankful for all food, it is Brahman. His universal energy is transmuted into our individual energy and helps us in all that we do.

Saturday, June 29, 1895.

(RECORDED BY MISS S. E. WALDO, A DISCIPLE)

(*The Swami came this morning with a Gita in his hand.*)

Krishna, the "Lord of souls", talks to Arjuna or Gudâkesha, "lord of sleep" (he who has conquered sleep). The "field of virtue" (the battlefield) is this world; the five brothers (representing righteousness) fight the hundred other brothers (all that we love and have to contend against); the most heroic brother, Arjuna (the awakened soul), is the general. We have to fight all sense-delights, the things to which we are most attached, to kill them. We have to stand alone; we are Brahman, all other ideas must be merged in this one.

Krishna did everything but without any attachment; he was in the world, but not of it. "Do all work but without attachment; work for work's sake, never for yourself."

Freedom can never be true of name and form; it is the clay out of which we (the pots) are made; then it is limited and not free, so that freedom can never be true of the related. One pot can never say "I am free" as a pot; only as it loses all ideas of form does it become free. The whole universe is only the Self with variations, the one tune made bearable by variation; sometimes there are discords, but they only make the subsequent harmony more perfect. In the universal melody three ideas stand out — freedom, strength, and sameness.

If your freedom hurts others, you are not free there. You must not hurt others.

"To be weak is to be miserable", says Milton. Doing and suffering are inseparably joined. (Often, too, the man who laughs most is the one who suffers most.) "To work you have the right, not to the fruits thereof."

* * *

Evil thoughts, looked at materially, are the disease bacilli.

Each thought is a little hammer blow on the lump of iron which our bodies are, manufacturing out of it what we want it to be.

We are heirs to all the good thoughts of the universe, if we open ourselves to them.

The book is all in us. Fool, hearest not thou? In thine own heart day and night is singing that Eternal Music — *Sachchidânanda, soham, soham* — Existence-Knowledge-Bliss Absolute, I am He, I am He.

The fountain of all knowledge is in every one of us, in the ant as in the highest angel. Real religion is one, but we quarrel with the forms, the symbols, the illustrations. The millennium exists already for those who find it; we have lost ourselves and then think the world is lost.

Perfect strength will have no activity in this world; it only is, it does not act.

While real perfection is only one, relative perfections must be many.

Sunday, June 30, 1895.

(RECORDED BY MISS S. E. WALDO, A DISCIPLE)

To try to think without a phantasm is to try to make the impossible possible. We cannot think "mammalia" without a concrete example. So with the idea of God.

The great abstraction of ideas in the world is what we call God.

Each thought has two parts — the thinking and the word; and we must have both. Neither idealists nor materialists are right; we must take both idea and expression.

All knowledge is of the reflected, as we can only see our face in a mirror. No one will ever know his own Self or God; but we are that own Self, we are God.

In Nirvana you are when *you* are not. Buddha said, "You are best, you are real, when you are not" — when the little self is gone.

The Light Divine within is obscured in most people. It is like a lamp in a cask of iron, no gleam of light can shine through. Gradually, by purity and unselfishness we can make the obscuring medium less and less dense, until at last it becomes as transparent as glass. Shri Ramakrishna was like the iron cask transformed into a glass cask through which can be seen the inner light as it is. We are all on the way to become the cask of glass and even higher and higher reflections. As long as there is a "cask" at all, we must think through material means. No impatient one can ever succeed.

* * *

Great saints are the object-lessons of the Principle. But the disciples make the saint the Principle, and then they forget the Principle in the person.

The result of Buddha's constant inveighing against a personal God was the introduction of idols into India. In the Vedas they knew them not, because they saw God everywhere, but the reaction against the loss of God as Creator and Friend was to make idols, and Buddha became an idol — so too with Jesus. The range of idols is from wood and stone to Jesus and Buddha, but we must have idols.

* * *

Violent attempts at reform always end by retarding reform. Do not say, "You are bad"; say only, "You are good, but be better."

Priests are an evil in every country, because they denounce and criticise, pulling at one string to mend it until two or three others are out of place. Love never denounces, only ambition does that. There is no such thing as "righteous" anger or justifiable killing.

If you do not allow one to become a lion, he will become a fox. Women are a power, only now it is more for evil because man oppresses woman; she is the fox, but when she is not longer oppressed, she will become the lion.

Ordinarily speaking, spiritual aspiration ought to be balanced through the intellect; otherwise it may degenerate into mere sentimentality. . . .

All theists agree that behind the changeable there is an Unchangeable, though they vary in their conception of the Ultimate. Buddha denied this *in toto*. "There is no Brahman, no Atman, no soul," he said.

As a character Buddha was the greatest the world has ever seen; next to him Christ. But the teachings of Krishna as taught by the Gita are the grandest the world has ever known. He who wrote that wonderful poem was one of those rare souls whose lives sent a wave of regeneration through the world. The human race will never again see such a brain as his who wrote the Gita.

* * *

There is only one Power, whether manifesting as evil or good. God and the devil are the same river with the water flowing in opposite directions.

Monday, July 1, 1895.

(RECORDED BY MISS S. E. WALDO, A DISCIPLE)

(Shri Ramakrishna Deva)

Shri Ramakrishna was the son of a very orthodox Brahmin, who would refuse even a gift from any but a special caste of Brahmins; neither might he work, nor even be a priest in a temple, nor sell books, nor serve anyone. He could only have "what fell from the skies" (alms), and even then it must not come through a "fallen" Brahmin. Temples have no hold on the Hindu religion; if they were all destroyed, religion would not be affected a grain. A man must only build a house for "God and guests", to build for himself would be selfish; therefore he erects temples as dwelling places for God.

Owing to the extreme poverty of his family, Shri Ramakrishna was obliged to become in his boyhood a priest in a temple dedicated to the Divine Mother, also called Prakriti, or Kâli, represented by a female figure standing with feet on a male figure, indicating that until Maya lifts, we can know nothing. Brahman is neuter, unknown and unknowable, but to be objectified He covers Himself with a veil of Maya, becomes the Mother of the Universe, and so brings forth the creation. The prostrate figure (Shiva or God) has become Shava (dead or lifeless) by being covered by Maya. The Jnâni says, "I will uncover God by force" (Advaitism); but the dualist says, "I will uncover God by praying to Mother, begging Her to open the door to which She alone has the key."

The daily service of the Mother Kali gradually awakened such intense devotion in the heart of the young priest that he could no longer carry on the regular temple worship. So he abandoned his duties and retired to a small woodland in the temple compound, where he gave himself up entirely to meditation. These woods were on the bank of the river Ganga; and one day the swift current bore to his very feet just the necessary materials to build him a little enclosure. In this enclosure he stayed and wept and prayed, taking no thought for the care of his body or for aught except his Divine Mother. A relative fed him once a day and watched over him. Later came a Sannyasini or lady ascetic, to help him find his "Mother". Whatever teachers he needed came to him unsought; from every sect some holy saint would come and offer to teach him and to each he listened eagerly. But he worshipped only Mother; all to him was Mother.

Shri Ramakrishna never spoke a harsh word against anyone. So beautifully tolerant was he that every sect thought that he belonged to them. He loved everyone. To him all religions were true. He found a place for each one. He was free, but free in love, not in "thunder". The mild type creates, the thundering type spreads. Paul was the thundering type to spread the light. (And it has been said by many that Swami Vivekananda himself was a kind of St. Paul to Shri Ramakrishna.)

The age of St. Paul, however, is gone; we are to be the new lights for this day. A self-adjusting organisation is the great need of our time. When we can get one, that will be the last religion of the world. The wheel must turn, and we should help it, not hinder. The waves of religious thought rise and fall, and on the topmost one stands the "prophet of the period". Ramakrishna came to teach the religion of today, constructive, not destructive. He had to go afresh to Nature to ask for facts, and he got scientific religion which never says "believe", but "see"; "I see, and you too can see." Use the same means and you will reach the same vision. God will come to everyone, harmony is within the reach of all. Shri Ramakrishna's teachings are "the gist of Hinduism"; they were not peculiar to him. Nor did he claim that they were; he cared naught for name or fame.

He began to preach when he was about forty; but he never went out to do it. He waited for those who wanted his teachings to come to him. In accordance with Hindu custom, he was married by his parents in early youth to a little girl of five, who remained at home with her family in a distant village, unconscious of the great struggle through which her young husband was passing. When she reached maturity, he was already deeply absorbed in religious devotion. She travelled on foot from her home to the temple at Dakshineswar where he was then living; and as soon as she saw him, she recognised what he was, for she herself was a great soul, pure and holy, who only desired to help his work, never to drag him down to the level of the Grihastha (householder).

Shri Ramakrishna is worshipped in India as one of the great Incarnations, and his birthday is celebrated there as a religious festival. . . .

A curious round stone is the emblem of Vishnu, the omnipresent. Each morning a priest comes in, offers sacrifice to the idol, waves incense before it, then puts it to bed and apologises to God for worshipping Him in that way, because he can only conceive of Him through an image or by means of some material object. He bathes the idol, clothes it, and puts his divine self into the idol "to make it alive".

* * *

There is a sect which says, "It is weakness to worship only the good and beautiful, we ought also to love and worship the hideous and the evil." This sect prevails all over Tibet, and they have no marriage. In India proper they cannot exist openly, but organise secret societies. No decent men will belong to them except *sub rosa*. Thrice communism was tried in Tibet, and thrice it failed. They use Tapas and with immense success as far as power is concerned.

Tapas means literally "to burn". It is a kind of penance to "heat" the higher nature. It is sometimes in the form of a sunrise to sunset vow, such as repeating Om all day incessantly. These actions will produce a certain power that you can convert into any form you wish, spiritual or material. This idea of Tapas penetrates the whole of Hindu religion. The Hindus even say that God made Tapas to create the world. It is a mental instrument with which to do everything. "Everything in the three worlds can be caught by Tapas." . . .

People who report about sects with which they are not in sympathy are both conscious and unconscious liars. A believer in one sect can rarely see truth in others.

* * *

A great Bhakta (Hanuman) once said when asked what day of the month it was, "God is my eternal date, no other date I care for."

Tuesday, July 2, 1895.

(RECORDED BY MISS S. E. WALDO, A DISCIPLE)

(*The Divine Mother.*)

Shâktas worship the Universal Energy as Mother, the sweetest name they know; for the mother is the highest ideal of womanhood in India. When God is worshipped as "Mother", as Love, the Hindus call it the "right-handed" way, and it leads to spirituality but never to material prosperity. When God is worshipped on His terrible side, that is, in the "left-handed" way, it leads usually to great material prosperity, but rarely to spirituality; and eventually it leads to degeneration and the obliteration of the race that practices it.

Mother is the first manifestation of power and is considered a higher idea than father. With the name of Mother comes the idea of Shakti, Divine Energy and Omnipotence, just as the baby believes its mother to be all-powerful, able to do anything. The Divine Mother is the Kundalini ("coiled up" power) sleeping in us; without worshipping Her we can never know ourselves. All-merciful, all-powerful, omnipresent are attributes of Divine Mother. She is the sum total of the energy in the universe. Every manifestation of power in the universe is "Mother". She is life, She is intelligence, She is Love. She is in the universe yet separate from it. She is a person and can be seen and known (as Shri Ramakrishna saw and knew Her). Established in the idea of Mother, we can do anything. She quickly answers prayer.

She can show; Herself to us in any form at any moment. Divine Mother can have form (Rupa) and name (Nâma) or name without form; and as we worship Her in these various aspects we can rise to pure Being, having neither form nor name.

The sum total of all the cells in an organism is one person; so each soul is like one cell and the sum of them is God, and beyond that is the Absolute. The sea calm is the Absolute; the same sea in waves is Divine Mother.

She is time, space, and causation. God is Mother and has two natures, the conditioned and the unconditioned. As the former, She is God, nature, and soul (man). As the latter, She is unknown and unknowable. Out of the Unconditioned came the trinity — God, nature, and soul, the triangle of existence. This is the Vishishtâdvaitist idea.

A bit of Mother, a drop, was Krishna, another was Buddha, another was Christ. The worship of even one spark of Mother in our earthly mother leads to greatness. Worship Her if you want love and wisdom.

Wednesday,July 3, 1895.

(RECORDED BY MISS S. E. WALDO, A DISCIPLE)

Generally speaking, human religion begins with fear. "The fear of the Lord is the beginning of wisdom." But later comes the higher idea. "Perfect love casteth out fear." Traces of fear will remain with us until we get knowledge, know what God is. Christ, being man, had to see impurity and denounced it; but God, infinitely higher, does not see iniquity and cannot be angry. Denunciation is never the highest. David's hands were smeared with blood; he could not build the temple. (Bible, Samuel, Chap. XVII — end.)

The more we grow in love and virtue and holiness, the more we see love and virtue and holiness outside. All condemnation of others really condemns ourselves. Adjust the microcosm (which is in your power to do) and the macrocosm will adjust itself for you. It is like the *hydrostatic paradox*, one drop of water can balance the universe. We cannot see outside what we are not inside. The universe is to us what the huge engine is to the miniature engine; and indication of any error in the tiny engine leads us to imagine trouble in the huge one.

Every step that has been really gained in the world has been gained by love; criticising can never do any good, it has been tried for thousand of years. Condemnation accomplishes nothing.

A real Vedantist must sympathise with all. Monism, or absolute oneness is the very soul of Vedanta. Dualists naturally tend to become intolerant, to think theirs as the only way. The Vaishnavas in India, who are dualists, are a most intolerant sect. Among the Shaivas, another dualistic sect, the story is told of a devotee by the name of Ghantâkarna or the Bell-eared, who was so devout a worshipper of Shiva that he did not wish even to hear the name of any other deity; so he wore two bells tied to his ears in order to drown the sound of any voice uttering other Divine names. On account of his intense devotion to Shiva, the latter wanted to teach him that there was no difference between Shiva and Vishnu, so He appeared before him as half Vishnu and half Shiva. At that moment the devotee was waving incense before Him, but so great was the bigotry of Ghantakarna that when he saw the fragrance of the incense entering the nostril of Vishnu, he thrust his finger into it to prevent the god from enjoying the sweet smell. . . .

The meat-eating animal, like the lion, gives one blow and *subsides*, but the patient bullock goes on all day, eating and sleeping as it walks. The "live Yankee" cannot compete with the rice-eating Chinese coolie. While military power dominates, meat-eating still prevail; but with the advance of science, fighting will grow less, and then the vegetarians will come in.

* * *

We divide ourselves into two to love God, myself loving my Self. God has created me and I have created God. We create God in our image; it is we who create Him to be our master, it is not God who makes us His servants. When we know that we are one with God, that we and He are friends, then come equality and freedom. So long as you hold yourself separated by a hair's breadth from this Eternal One, fear cannot go.

Never ask that foolish question, what good will it do to the world? Let the world go. Love and ask nothing; love and look for nothing further. Love and forget all the "isms". Drink the cup of love and become mad. Say "Thine, O Thine for ever O Lord!" and plunge in, forgetting all else. The very idea of God is love. Seeing a cat loving her kittens stand and pray. God has become manifest there; literally believe this. Repeat "I am Thine, I am Thine", for we can see God everywhere. Do not seek for Him, just see Him.

"May the Lord ever keep you alive, Light of the world, Soul of the universe!" . . .

The Absolute cannot be worshipped, so we must worship a manifestation, such a one as has our nature. Jesus had our nature; he became the Christ; so can we, and so *must* we. Christ and Buddha were the names of a state to be attained; Jesus and Gautama were the persons to manifest it. "Mother" is the first and highest manifestation, next the Christs and Buddhas. We make our own environment, and we strike the fetters off. The Atman is the fearless. When we pray to a God outside, it is good, only we do not know what we do. When we know the Self, we understand. The highest expression of love is unification.

"There was a time when I was a woman and he was a man.

Still love grew until there was neither he nor I;

Only I remember faintly there was a time when there were two.

But love came between and made them one."

— *Persian Sufi Poem*

Knowledge exists eternally and is co-existent with God. The man who discovers a spiritual law is inspired, and what he brings is revelation; but revelation too is eternal, not to be crystallised as final and then blindly followed. The Hindus have been criticised so many years by their conquerors that they (the Hindus) dare to criticise their religion themselves, and this makes them free. Their foreign rulers struck off their fetters without knowing it. The most religious people on earth, the Hindus have actually no sense of blasphemy; to speak of holy things in any way is to them in itself a sanctification. Nor have they any artificial respect for prophets or books, or for hypocritical piety.

The Church tries to fit Christ into it, not the Church into Christ; so only those writings were preserved that suited the purpose in hand. Thus the books are not to be depended upon and book-worship is the worst kind of idolatry to bind our feet. All has to conform to the book — science, religion, philosophy; it is the most horrible tyranny, this tyranny of the Protestant Bible. Every man in Christian countries has a huge cathedral on his head and on top of that a book, and yet man lives and grows! Does not this prove that man is God?

Man is the highest being that exists, and this is the greatest world. We can have no conception of God higher than man, so our God is man, and man is God. When we rise and go beyond and find something higher, we have to jump out of the mind, out of body and the imagination and leave this world; when we rise to be the Absolute, we are no longer in this world. Man is the apex of the only world we can ever know. All we know of animals is only by analogy, we judge them by what we do and feel ourselves.

The sum total of knowledge is ever the same, only sometimes it is more manifested and sometimes less. The only source of it is within, and there only is it found.

* * *

All poetry, painting, and music is feeling expressed through words, through colour, through sound. . . .

Blessed are those upon whom their sins are quickly visited, their account is the sooner balanced! Woe to those whose punishment is deferred, it is the greater!

Those who have attained sameness are said to be living in God. All hatred is killing the "Self by the self", therefore love is the law of life. To rise to this is to be perfect; but the more perfect we are, less work (so-called) can we do. The Sâttvika see and know that all is mere child's play and do not trouble themselves about anything.

It is easy to strike a blow, but tremendously hard to stay the hand, stand still, and say, "In Thee, O Lord, I take refuge", and then wait for Him to act.

Friday, July 5, 1895.

(R ECORDED BY M ISS S. E. W
ALDO , A DISCIPLE)

Until you are ready to change any minute, you can never see the truth; but you must hold fast and be steady in the search for truth. . . .

Chârvâkas, a very ancient sect in India, were rank materialists. They have died out now, and most of their books are lost. They claimed that the soul, being the product of the body and its forces, died with it; that there was no proof of its further existence. They denied inferential knowledge accepting only perception by the senses.

* * *

Samâdhi is when the Divine and human are in one, or it is "bringing sameness". . . .

Materialism says, the voice of freedom is a delusion. Idealism says, the voice that tells of bondage is delusion. Vedanta says, you are free and not free at the same time — never free on the earthly plane, but ever free on the spiritual.

Be beyond both freedom and bondage.

We are Shiva, we are immortal knowledge beyond the senses.

Infinite power is back of everyone; pray to Mother, and it will come to you.

"O Mother, giver of Vâk (eloquence), Thou self-existent, come as the Vak upon my-lips," (Hindu invocation).

"That Mother whose voice is in the thunder, come Thou in me! Kali, Thou time eternal, Thou force irresistible, Shakti, Power!"

Saturday, July 6, 1895.

(RECORDED BY MISS S. E. WALDO, A DISCIPLE)

*(Today we had Shankaracharya's commentary
on Vyâsa's Vedânta Sutras.)*

Om tat sat! According to Shankara, there are two phases of the universe, one is I and the other thou; and they are as contrary as light and darkness, so it goes without saying that neither can be derived from the other. On the subject, the object has been superimposed; the subject is the only reality, the other a mere appearance. The opposite view is untenable. Matter and the external world are but the soul in a certain state; in reality there is only one.

All our world comes from truth and untruth coupled together. Samsâra (life) is the result of the contradictory forces acting upon us, like the diagonal motion of a ball in a parallelogram of forces. The world is God and is real, but that is not the world we see; just as we see silver in the mother-of-pearl where it is not. This is what is known as Adhyâsa or superimposition, that is, a relative existence dependent upon a real one, as when we recall a scene we have seen; for the time it exists for us, but that existence is not real. Or some say, it is as when we imagine heat in water, which does not belong to it; so really it is something which has been put where it does not belong, "taking the thing for what it is not". We see reality, but distorted by the medium through which we see it.

You can never know yourself except as objectified. When we mistake one thing for another, we always take the thing before us as the real, never the unseen; thus we mistake the object for the subject. The Atman never becomes the object. Mind is the internal sense, the outer senses are its instruments. In the subject is a trifle of the objectifying power that enables him to know "I am"; but the subject is the object of its own Self, never of the mind or the senses. You can, however, superimpose one idea on another idea, as when we say, "The sky is blue", the sky itself being only an idea. Science and nescience there are, but the Self is never affected by any nescience. Relative knowledge is good, because it leads to absolute knowledge; but neither the knowledge of the senses, nor of the mind, nor even of the Vedas is true, since they are all within the realm of relative knowledge. First get rid of the delusion, "I am the body", then only can we want real knowledge. Man's knowledge is only a higher degree of brute knowledge.

* * *

One part of the Vedas deals with Karma — form and ceremonies. The other part deals with the knowledge of Brahman and discusses religion. The Vedas in this part teach of the Self; and because they do, their knowledge is approaching real knowledge. Knowledge of the Absolute depends upon no book, nor upon anything; it is absolute in itself. No amount of study will give this knowledge; is not theory, it is realization. Cleanse the dust from the mirror, purify your own mind, and in a flash you know that you are Brahman.

God exists, not birth nor death, not pain nor misery, nor murder, nor change, nor good nor evil; all is Brahman. We take the "rope for the serpent", the error is ours. . . . We can only do good when we love God and He reflects our love. The murderer is God, and the "clothing of murderer" is only superimposed upon him. Take him by the hand and tell him the truth.

Soul has no caste, and to think it has is a delusion; so are life and death, or any motion or quality. The Atman never changes, never goes nor comes. It is the eternal Witness of all Its own manifestations, but we take It for the manifestation; an eternal illusion, without beginning or end, ever going on. The Vedas, however, have to come down to our level, for if they told us the highest truth in the highest way, we could not understand it.

Heaven is a mere superstition arising from desire, and desire is ever a yoke, a degeneration. Never approach any thing except as God; for if we do, we see evil, because we throw a veil of delusion over what we look at, and then we see evil. Get free from these illusions; be blessed. Freedom is to lose all illusions.

In one sense Brahman is known to every human being; he knows, "I am"; but man does not know himself as he is. We all know we are, but not how we are. All lower explanations are partial truths; but the flower, the essence of the Vedas, is that the Self in each of us is Brahman. Every phenomenon is included in birth, growth, and death — appearance, continuance and disappearance. Our own realisation is beyond the Vedas, because even they depend upon that. The highest Vedanta is the philosophy of the Beyond.

To say that creation has any beginning is to lay the axe at the root of all philosophy.

Maya is the energy of the universe, potential and kinetic. Until Mother releases us, we cannot get free.

The universe is ours to enjoy. But want nothing. To want is weakness. Want makes us beggars, and we are sons of the king, not beggars.

Sunday, July 7, 1895.

Infinite manifestation dividing itself in portion still remains infinite, and each portion is infinite.

Brahman is the same in two forms — changeable and unchangeable, expressed and unexpressed. Know that the Knower and the known are one. The Trinity — the Knower, the known, and knowing — is manifesting as this universe. That God the Yogi sees in meditation, he sees through the power of his own Self.

What we call nature, fate, is simply God's will.

So long as enjoyment is sought, bondage remains. Only imperfection can enjoy, because enjoyment is the fulfilling of desire. The human soul enjoys nature. The underlying reality of nature, soul, and God is Brahman; but It (Brahman) is unseen, until we bring It out. It may be brought out by *Pramantha* or friction, just as we can produce fire by friction. The body is the lower piece of wood, Om is the pointed piece and Dhyâna (meditation) is the friction. When this is used, that light which is the knowledge of Brahman will burst forth in the soul. Seek it through Tapas. Holding the body upright, sacrifice the organs of sense in the mind. The sense-centres are within, and their organs without; drive them into the mind and through Dhârâna (concentration) fix the mind in Dhyana. Brahman is omnipresent in the universe as is butter in milk, but friction makes It manifest in one place. As churning brings out the butter in the milk, so Dhyana brings the realisation of Brahman in the soul.

All Hindu philosophy declares that there is a sixth sense, the superconscious, and through it comes inspiration.

* * *

The universe is motion, and friction will eventually bring everything to an end; then comes a rest; and after that all begins again. . . .

So long as the "skin sky" surrounds man, that is, so long as he identifies himself with his body, he cannot see God.

Sunday AFTERNOON

There are six schools of philosophy in India that are regarded as orthodox, because they believe in the Vedas.

Vyasa's philosophy is *par excellence* that of the Upanishads. He wrote in Sutra form, that is, in brief algebraical symbols without nominative or verb. This caused so much ambiguity that out of the Sutras came dualism, mono-dualism, and monism or "roaring Vedanta"; and all the great commentators in these different schools were at times "conscious liars" in order to make the texts suit their philosophy.

The Upanishads contain very little history of the doings of any man, but nearly all other scriptures are largely personal histories. The Vedas deal almost entirely with philosophy. Religion without philosophy runs into superstition; philosophy without religion becomes dry atheism.

Vishishta-advaita is qualified Advaita (monism). Its expounder was Râmânuja. He says, "Out of the ocean of milk of the Vedas, Vyasa has churned this butter of philosophy, the better to help mankind." He says again, "All virtues and all qualities belong to Brahman, Lord of the universe. He is the greatest Purusha. Madhva is a through-going dualist or Dvaitist. He claims that even women might study the Vedas. He quotes chiefly from the Purânas. He says that Brahman means Vishnu, not Shiva at all, because there is no salvation except through Vishnu.

Monday, July 8, 1895.

(RECORDED BY MISS S. E. WALDO, A DISCIPLE)

There is no place for reasoning in Madhva's explanation, it is all taken from the revelation in the Vedas.

Ramanuja says, the Vedas are the holiest study. Let the sons of the three upper castes get the Sutra (The holy thread.) and at eight, ten, or eleven years of age begin the study, which means going to a Guru and learning the Vedas word for word, with perfect intonation and pronunciation.

Japa is repeating the Holy Name; through this the devotee rises to the Infinite. This boat of sacrifice and ceremonies is very frail, we need more than that to know Brahman, which alone is freedom. Liberty is nothing more than destruction of ignorance, and that can only go when we know Brahman. It is not necessary to go through all these ceremonials to reach the meaning of the Vedanta. Repeating Om is enough.

Seeing difference is the cause of all misery, and ignorance is the cause of seeing difference. That is why ceremonials are not needed, because they increase the idea of inequality; you practice them to get rid of something or to obtain something.

Brahman is without action, Atman is Brahman, and we are Atman; knowledge like this takes off all error. It must be heard, apprehended intellectually, and lastly realised. Cogitating is applying reason and establishing this knowledge in ourselves by reason. Realising is making it a part of our lives by constant thinking of it. This constant thought or Dhyana is as oil that pours in one unbroken line from vessel to vessel; Dhyana rolls the mind in this thought day and night and so helps us to attain to liberation. Think always "Soham, Soham"; this is almost as good as liberation. Say it day and night; realisation will come as the result of this continuous cogitation. This absolute and continuous remembrance of the Lord is what is meant by Bhakti.

This Bhakti is indirectly helped by all good works. Good thoughts and good works create less differentiation than bad ones; so indirectly they lead to freedom. Work, but give up the results to the Lord. Knowledge alone can make us perfect. He who follows the God of Truth with devotion, to him the God of Truth reveals Himself. . . . We are lamps, and our burning is what we call "life". When the supply of oxygen gives out, then the lamp must go out. All we can do is to keep the lamp clean. Life is a product, a compound, and as such must resolve itself into its elements.

Tuesday, July 9, 1895.

(RECORDED BY MISS S. E. WALDO, A DISCIPLE)

Man as Atman is really free; as man he is bound, changed by every physical condition. As man, he is a machine with an idea of freedom; but this human body is the best and the human mind the highest mind there is. When a man attains to the Atman state, he can take a body, making it to suit himself; he is above law. This is a statement and must be proved. Each one must prove it for himself; we may satisfy ourselves, but we cannot satisfy another. Râja-Yoga is the only science of religion that can be demonstrated; and only what I myself have proved by experience, do I teach. The full ripeness of reason is intuition, but intuition cannot antagonise reason.

Work purifies the heart and so leads to Vidyâ (wisdom). The Buddhists said, doing good to men and to animals were the only works; the Brahmins said that worship and all ceremonials were equally "work" and purified the mind. Shankara declares that "all works, good and bad, are against knowledge". Actions tending to ignorance are sins, not directly, but as causes, because they tend to increase Tamas and Rajas. With Sattva only, comes wisdom. Virtuous deeds take off the veil from knowledge, and knowledge alone can make us see God.

Knowledge can never be created, it can only be discovered; and every man who makes a great discovery is inspired. Only, when it is a spiritual truth he brings, we call him a prophet; and when it is on the physical plane, we call him a scientific man, and we attribute more importance to the former, although the source of all truth is one.

Shankara says, Brahman is the *essence, the reality of all knowledge,* and that all manifestations as knower, knowing, and known are mere imaginings in Brahman. Ramanuja attributes consciousness to God; the real monists attribute nothing, not even existence in any meaning that we can attach to it. Ramanuja declares that God is the essence of conscious knowledge. Undifferentiated consciousness, when differentiated, becomes the world. . .

Buddhism, one of the most philosophical religions in the world, spread all through the populace, the common people of India. What a wonderful culture there must have been among the Aryans twenty-five hundred years ago, to be able to grasp ideas!

Buddha was the only great Indian philosopher who would not recognise caste, and not one of his followers remains in India. All the other philosophers pandered more or less to social prejudices; no matter how high they soared, still a bit of the vulture remained in them. As my Master used to say, "The vulture soars high out of sight in the sky, but his eye is ever on a bit of carrion on the earth."

* * *

The ancient Hindus were wonderful scholars, veritable living encyclopaedias. They said, "Knowledge in books and money in other people's hands is like no knowledge and no money at all."

Shankara was regarded by many as an incarnation of Shiva.

Wednesday, July 10, 1895.

(RECORDED BY MISS S. E. WALDO, A DISCIPLE)

There are sixty-five million Mohammedans in India, some of them Sufis. Sufis identify man with God, and through them this idea came into Europe. They say, "I am that Truth"; but they have an *esoteric* as well as an *exoteric* doctrine, although Mohammed himself did not hold it.

"*Hashshashin*" has become our word "assassin", because an old sect of Mohammedanism killed nonbelievers as a part of its creed.

A pitcher of water has to be present in the Mohammedan worship as a symbol of God filling the universe.

The Hindus believe that there will be ten Divine Incarnations. Nine have been and the tenth is still to come.

* * *

Shankara sometimes resorts to sophistry in order to prove that the ideas in the books go to uphold his philosophy. Buddha was more brave and sincere than any teacher. He said: "Believe no book; the Vedas are all humbug. If they agree with me, so much the better for the books. I am the greatest book; sacrifice and prayer are useless." Buddha was the first human being to give to the world a complete system of morality. He was good for good's sake, he loved for love's sake.

Shankara says: God is to be reasoned on, because the Vedas say so. Reason helps inspiration; books and realised reason — or individualized perception — both are proofs of God. The Vedas are, according to him, a sort of incarnation of universal knowledge. The proof of God is that He brought forth the Vedas, and the proof of the Vedas is that such wonderful books could only have been given out by Brahman. They are the mine of all knowledge, and they have come out of Him as a man breathes out air; therefore we know that He is infinite in power and knowledge. He may or may not have created the world, that is a trifle; to have produced the Vedas is more important! The world has come to know God through the Vedas; no other way there is.

And so universal is this belief, held by Shankara, in the all-inclusiveness of the Vedas that there is even a Hindu proverb that if a man loses his cow, he goes to look for her in the Vedas!

Shankara further affirms that obedience to ceremonial is not knowledge. Knowledge of God is independent of moral duties, or sacrifice or ceremonial, or what we think or do not think, just as the stump is not affected when one man takes it for a ghost and another sees it as it is.

Vedanta is necessary because neither reasoning nor books can show us God. He is only to be realised by superconscious perception, and Vedanta teaches how to attain that. You must get beyond personal God (Ishvara) and reach the Absolute Brahman. God is the perception of every being: He is all there is to he perceived. That which says "I" is Brahman, but although we, day and night, perceive Him; we do not know that we are perceiving Him. As soon as we become aware of this truth, all misery goes; so we must get knowledge of the truth. Reach unity; no more duality will come. But knowledge does not come by sacrifice, but by seeking, worshipping, knowing the Atman.

Brahmavidyâ is the highest knowledge, knowing the Brahman; lower knowledge is science. This is the teaching of the Mundakopanishad or the Upanishad for Sannyâsins. There are two sorts of knowledge — principal and secondary. The unessential is that part of the Vedas dealing with worship and ceremonial, also all secular knowledge. The essential is that by which we reach the Absolute. It (the Absolute) creates all from Its own nature; there is nothing to cause, nothing outside. It is all energy, It is all there is. He who makes all sacrifices to himself, the Atman, he alone knows Brahman. Fools think outside worship the highest; fools think works can give us God. Only those who go through the Sushumnâ (the "path" of the Yogis) reach the Atman. They must go to a Guru to learn. Each part has the same nature as the whole; all springs from the Atman. Meditation is the arrow, the whole soul going out to God is the bow, which speeds the arrow to its mark, the Atman. As finite, we can never express the Infinite, but we are the Infinite. Knowing this we argue with no one.

Divine wisdom is to be got by devotion, meditation, and chastity. "Truth alone triumphs, and not untruth. Through truth alone the way is spread to Brahman" — where alone love and truth are.

Thursday, July 11, 1895.

(RECORDED BY MISS S. E. WALDO, A DISCIPLE)

Without mother-love no creation could continue. Nothing is entirely physical, nor yet entirely metaphysical; one presupposes the other and explains the other. All Theists agree that there is a background to this visible universe, they differ as to the nature or character of that background. Materialists say there is no background.

In all religions the superconscious state is identical. Hindus, Christians, Mohammedans, Buddhists, and even those of no creed, all have the very same experience when they transcend the body. . . .

The purest Christians in the world were established in India by the Apostle Thomas about twenty-five years after the death of Jesus. This was while the Anglo-Saxons were still savages, painting their bodies and living in caves. The Christians in India once numbered about three millions, but now there are about one million.

Christianity is always propagated by the sword. How wonderful that the disciples of such a gentle soul should kill so much! The three missionary religions are the Buddhist, Mohammedan, and Christian. The three older ones, Hinduism, Judaism and Zoroastrianism, never sought to make converts. Buddhists never killed, but converted three-quarters of the world at one time by pure gentleness.

The Buddhists were the most logical agnostics. You can really stop nowhere between nihilism and absolutism. The Buddhists were intellectually all-destroyers, carrying their theory to its ultimate logical issue. The Advaitists also worked out their theory to its logical conclusion and reached the Absolute — one identified Unit Substance out of which all phenomena are being manifested. Both Buddhists and Advaitists have a feeling of identity and non-identity at the same time; one of these feelings must be false, and the other true. The nihilist puts the reality in non-identity, the realist puts the reality in identity; and this is the fight which occupies the whole world. This is the "tug-of-war".

The realist asks, "How does the nihilist get any idea of identity?" How does the revolving light appear a circle? A point of rest alone explains motion. The nihilist can never explain the genesis of the delusion that there is a background; neither can the idealist explain how the One becomes the many. The only explanation must come from beyond the sense-plane; we must rise to the superconscious, to a state entirely beyond sense-perception. That metaphysical power is the further instrument that the idealist alone can use. He can experience the Absolute; the man Vivekananda can resolve himself into the Absolute and then come back to the man again. For him, then the problem is solved and secondarily for others, for he can show the way to others. Thus religion begins where philosophy ends. The "good of the world" will be that what is now superconscious for us will in ages to come be the conscious for all. Religion is therefore the highest work the world has; and because man has unconsciously felt this, he has clung through all the ages to the idea of religion.

Religion, the great milch cow, has given many kicks, but never mind, it gives a great deal of milk. The milkman does not mind the kick of the cow which gives much milk. Religion is the greatest child to be born, the great "moon of realisation"; let us feed it and help it grow, and it will become a giant. King Desire and King Knowledge fought, and just as the latter was about to be defeated, he was reconciled to Queen Upanishad and a child was born to him, Realisation, who saved the victory to him.(From the *Prabodha-chandrodaya*, a Vedantic Sanskrit masque.)

Love concentrates all the power of the will without effort, as when a man falls in love with a woman.

The path of devotion is natural and pleasant. Philosophy is taking the mountain stream back to its force. It is a quicker method but very hard. Philospophy says, "Check everything." Devotion says, "Give the stream, have eternal self-surrender." It is a longer way, but easier and happier.

"Thine am I for ever; henceforth whatever I do, it is Thou doing it. No more is there any me or mine."

"Having no money to give, no brains to learn, no time to practice Yoga, to Thee, O sweet One, I give myself, to Thee my body and mind."

No amount of ignorance or wrong ideas can put a barrier between the soul and God. Even if there be no God, still hold fast to love. It is better to die seeking a God than as a dog seeking only carrion. Choose the highest ideal, and give your life up to that. "Death being so certain, it is the highest thing to give up life for a great purpose."

Love will painlessly attain to philosophy; then after knowledge comes Parâbhakti (supreme devotion).

Knowledge is critical and makes a great fuss over everything; but Love says, "God will show His real nature to me" and accepts all.

RABBIA

Rabbia, sick upon her bed,
By two saints was visited —
Holy Malik, Hassan wise —
Men of mark in Moslem eyes.

Hassan said, "Whose prayer is pure
Will God's chastisements endure."
Malik, from a deeper sense
Uttered his experience:
"He who loves his master's choice
Will in chastisement *rejoice.*"

Rabbia saw some selfish will
In their maxims lingering still,
And replied "O men of grace,
He who sees his Master's face,
Will not in his prayers recall
That he is chastised at all !"

— *Persian Poem*

Friday, July 12, 1895.

(R ECORDED BY M ISS S. E. W
ALDO , A DISCIPLE)

(*Shankara's Commentary*.)

Fourth Vyasa Sutra. "Âtman (is) the aim of all."

Ishvara is to be known from the Vedanta; all Vedas point to Him (Who is the Cause; the Creator, Preserver and Destroyer). Ishvara is the unification of the Trinity, known as Brahmâ, Vishnu, and Shiva, which stand at the head of the Hindu Pantheon. "Thou art our Father who takest us to the other shore of the dark ocean" (Disciple's words to the Master).

The Vedas cannot show you Brahman, you are That already; they can only help to take away the veil that hides the truth from our eyes. The first veil to vanish is ignorance; and when that is gone, sin goes; next desire ceases, selfishness ends, and all misery disappears. This cessation of ignorance can only come when I know that God and I are one; in other words, identify yourself with Atman, not with human limitations. *Dis*-identify yourself with the body, and all pain will cease. This is the secret of healing. The universe is a case of hypnotisation; de-hypnotise yourself and cease to suffer.

In order to be free we have to pass through vice to virtue, and then get rid of both. Tamas is to be conquered by Rajas, both are to be submerged in Sattva; then go beyond the three qualities. Reach a state where your very breathing is a prayer.

Whenever you learn (gain anything) from another man's words, know that you had the experience in a previous existence, because experience is the only teacher.

With all powers comes further misery, so kill desire. Getting any desire is like putting a stick into a nest of hornets. Vairâgya is finding, out that desires are but gilded balls of poison.

"Mind is not God" (Shankara). "Tat tvam asi" "Aham Brahmâsmi" ("That thou art", "I am Brahman"). When a man realises this, all the knots of his heart are cut asunder, all his doubts vanish". Fearlessness is not possible as long as we have even God *over us*; we must *be* God. What is disjoined will be for ever disjoined; if you are separate from God, then you can never be one with Him, and vice versa. If by virtue you are joined to God, when that ceases, disjunction will come. The junction is eternal, and virtue only helps to remove the veil. We are *âzâd* (free), we must realise it. "Whom the Self chooses" means we are the Self and choose ourselves.

Does seeing depend upon our own efforts or does it depend upon something outside? It depends upon ourselves; our efforts take off the dust, the mirror does not change. There is neither knower, knowing, nor known. "He who knows that he does not know, knows It." He who has a theory knows nothing.

The idea that we are bound is only an illusion.

Religion is not of this world; it is "heart-cleansing", and its effect on this world is secondary. Freedom is inseparable from the nature of the Atman. This is ever pure, ever perfect, ever unchangeable. This Atman you can never know. We can say nothing about the Atman but "not this, not this".

"Brahman is that which we can never drive out by any power of mind or imagination." (Shankara).

* * *

The universe is thought, and the Vedas are the words of this thought. We can create and uncreate this whole universe. Repeating the words, the unseen thought is aroused, and as a result a seen effect is produced. This is the claim of a certain sect of Karmis. They think that each one of us is a creator. Pronounce the words, the thought which corresponds will arise, and the result will become visible. "Thought is the power of the word, the word is the expression of the thought," say Mimâmsakas, a Hindu philosophical sect.

Saturday, July 13th, 1895.

Everything we know is a compound, and all sense-knowledge comes through analysis. To think that mind is a simple, single, or independent is dualism. Philosophy is not got by studying books; the more you read books, the more muddled becomes the mind. The idea of unthinking philosophers was that the mind was a simple, and this led them to believe in free-will. Psychology, the analysis of the mind, shows the mind to be a compound, and every compound must be held together by some outside force; so the will is bound by the combination of outside forces. Man cannot even will to eat unless he is hungry. Will is subject to desire. But we are free; everyone feels it.

The agnostic says this idea is a delusion. Then, how do you prove the world? Its only proof is that we all see it and feel it; so just as much we all feel freedom. If universal consensus affirms this world, then it must be accepted as affirming freedom; but freedom is not of the will as it is. The constitutional belief of man in freedom is the basis of all reasoning. Freedom is of the will as it was before it became bound. The very idea of free-will shows every moment man's struggle against bondage. The free can be only one, the Unconditioned, the Infinite, the Unlimited. Freedom in man is now a memory, an attempt towards freedom.

Everything in the universe is struggling to complete a circle, to return to its source, to return to its only real Source, Atman. The search for happiness is a struggle to find the balance, to restore the equilibrium. Morality is the struggle of the bound will to get free and is the proof that we have come from perfection. . . .

The idea of duty is the midday sun of misery scorching the very soul. "O king, drink this one drop of nectar and be happy." ("I am not the doer", this is the nectar.)

Let there be action without reaction; action is pleasant, all misery is reaction. The child puts its hand in the flame, that is pleasure; but when its system reacts, then comes the pain of burning. When we can stop that reaction, then we have nothing to fear. Control the brain and do not let it read the record; be the witness and do not react, only thus can you be happy. The happiest moments we ever know are when we entirely forget ourselves. Work of your own free will, not from duty. We have no duty. This world is just a gymnasium in which we play; our life is an eternal holiday.

The whole secret of existence is to have no fear. Never fear what will become of you, depend on no one. Only the moment you reject all help are you free. The full sponge can absorb no more.

* * *

Even fighting in self-defence is wrong, though it is higher than fighting in aggression. There is no "righteous" indignation, because indignation comes from not recognising sameness in all things.

Sunday, July 14, 1895.

(RECORDED BY MISS S. E. WALDO, A DISCIPLE)

Philosophy in India means that through which we see God, the rationale of religion; so no Hindu could ever ask for a link between religion and philosophy.

Concrete, generalised, abstract are the three stages in the process of philosophy. The highest abstraction in which all things agree is the One. In religion we have first, symbols and forms; next, mythologies; and last, philosophy. The first two are for the time being; philosophy is the underlying basis of all, and the others are only stepping stones in the struggle to reach the Ultimate.

In Western religion the idea is that without the New Testament and Christ there could be no religion. A similar belief exists in Judaism with regard to Moses and the Prophets, because these religions are dependent upon mythology only. Real religion, the highest, rises above mythology; it can never rest upon that. Modern science has really made the foundations of religion strong. That the whole universe is one, is scientifically demonstrable. What the metaphysicians call "being", the physicist calls "matter", but there is no real fight between the two, for both are one. Though an atom is invisible, unthinkable, yet in it are the whole power and potency of the universe. That is exactly what the Vedantist says of Atman. All sects are really saying the same thing in different words.

Vedanta and modern science both posit a self-evolving Cause. In Itself are all the causes. Take for example the potter shaping a pot. The potter is the primal cause, the clay the material cause, and the wheel the instrumental cause; but the Atman is all three. Atman is cause and manifestation too. The Vedantist says the universe is not real, it is only apparent. Nature is God seen through nescience. The Pantheists say, God has become nature or this world; the Advaitists affirm that God is appearing as this world, but He is not this world.

We can only know experience as a mental process, a fact in the mind as well as a mark in the brain. We cannot push the brain back or forward, but we can the mind; it can stretch over all time — past, present, and future; and so facts in the mind are eternally preserved. All facts are already generalised in mind, which is omnipresent.

Kant's great achievement was the discovery that "time, space, and causation are modes of thought," but Vedanta taught this ages ago and called it "Maya." Schopenhauer stands on reason only and rationalises the Vedas. . . . Shankara maintained the orthodoxy of the Vedas.

* * *

"Treeness" or the idea of "tree", found out among trees is knowledge, and the highest knowledge is One. . . .

Personal God is the last generalization of the universe, only hazy, not clear-cut and philosophic. . . .

Unity is self-evolving, out of which everything comes.

Physical science is to find out facts, metaphysics is the thread to bind the flowers into a bouquet. Every abstraction is metaphysical; even putting manure at the root of a tree involves a process of abstraction. . . .

Religion includes the concrete, the more generalized and the ultimate unity. Do not stick to particularisations. Get to the principle, to the One. . . .

Devils are machines of darkness, angels are machines of light; but both are machines. Man alone is alive. Break the machine, strike the balance and then man can become free. This is the only world where man can work out his salvation.

"Whom the Self chooses" is true. Election is true, but put it within. As an external and fatalistic doctrine, it is horrible.

Monday, July 15, 1895.

(RECORDED BY MISS S. E. WALDO, A DISCIPLE)

Where there is polyandry, as in Tibet, women are physically stronger than the men. When the English go there, these women carry large men up the mountains.

In Malabar, although of course polyandry does not obtain there, the women lead in everything. Exceptional cleanliness is apparent everywhere and there is the greatest impetus to learning. When I myself was in that country, I met many women who spoke good Sanskrit, while in the rest of India not one woman in a million can speak it. Mastery elevates, and servitude debases. Malabar has never been conquered either by the Portuguese or by the Mussulmans.

The Dravidians were a non-Aryan race of Central Asia who preceded the Aryans, and those of Southern India were the most civilised. Women with them stood higher than men. They subsequently divided, some going to Egypt, others to Babylonia, and the rest remaining in India.

Tuesday, July 16, 1895.

(RECORDED BY MISS S. E. WALDO, A DISCIPLE)

(Shankara)

The "unseen cause" (Or mass of subtle impressions.) leads us to sacrifice and worship, which in turn produce seen results; but to attain liberation we must first hear, then think or reason, and then meditate upon Brahman.

The result of works and the result of knowledge are two different things. "Do" and "Do not do" are the background of all morality, but they really belong only to the body and the mind. All happiness and misery are inextricably connected with the senses, and body is necessary to experience them. The higher the body, the higher the standard of virtue, even up to Brahma; but all have bodies. As long as there is a body, there must be pleasure and pain; only when one has got rid of the body can one escape them. The Atman is bodiless, says Shankara.

No law can make you free, you are free. Nothing can give you freedom, if you have it not already. The Atman is self-illumined. Cause and effect do not reach there, and this disembodiedness is freedom. Beyond what was, or is, or is to be, is Brahman. As an effect, freedom would have no value; it would be a compound, and as such would contain the seeds of bondage. It is the one real factor. Not to be attained, hut the real nature of the soul.

Work and worship, however, are necessary to take away the veil, to lift oh the bondage and illusion. They do not give us freedom; but all the same, without effort on our own part we do not open our eyes and see what we are. Shankara says further that Advaita-Vedanta is the crowning glory of the Vedas; hut the lower Vedas are also necessary, because they teach work and worship, and through these many come to the Lord. Others may come without any help but Advaita. Work and worship lead to the same result as Advaita.

Books cannot teach God, but they can destroy ignorance; their action is negative. To hold to the books and at the same time open the way to freedom is Shankara's great achievement. But after all, it is a kind of hair-splitting. Give man first the concrete, then raise him to the highest by slow degrees. This is the effort of the various religions and explains their existence and why each is suited to some stage of development. The very books are a part of the ignorance they help to dispel. Their duty is to drive out the ignorance that has come upon knowledge. "Truth shall drive out untruth." You are free and cannot he made so. So long as you have a creed, you have no God. "He who knows he knows, knows nothing." Who can know the Knower? There are two eternal facts in existence, God and the universe, the former unchangeable, the latter changeable. The world exists eternally. Where your mind cannot grasp the amount of change, you call it eternally. . . . You see the stone or the bas-relief on it, but not both at once; yet both are one.

* * *

Can you make yourself at rest even for a second? All Yogis say you can.
. . .

The greatest sin is to think yourself weak. No one is greater: realise you are Brahman. Nothing has power except what you give it. We are beyond the sun, the stars, the universe. Teach the Godhood of man. Deny evil, create none. Stand up and say, I am the master, the master of all. We forge the chain, and we alone can break it.

No action can give you freedom; only knowledge can make you free, Knowledge is irresistible; the mind cannot take it or reject it. When it comes the mind has to accept it; so it is not a work of the mind; only, its expression comes in the mind.

Work or worship is to bring you back to your own nature. It is an entire illusion that the Self is the body; so even while living here in the body, we can be free. The body has nothing in common with the Self. Illusion is taking the real for the unreal — not "nothing at all".

Wednesday, July 17, 1895.

Râmânuja divides the universe into Chit, Achit, and Ishvara — man, nature, and God; conscious, subconscious, and superconscious. Shankara, on the contrary, says that Chit, the soul, is the same as God. God *is* truth, *is* knowledge, *is* infinity; these are not qualities. Any thought of God is a qualification, and all that can be said of Him is "Om tat sat".

Shankara further asks, can you see existence separate from everything else? Where is the differentiation between two objects? Not in sense-perception, else all would be one in it. We have to perceive in sequence. In getting knowledge of what a thing is, we get also something which it is not. The differentiae are in the memory and are got by comparison with what is stored there. Difference is not in the nature of a thing, it is in the brain. Homogeneous one is outside, differentiae are inside (in the mind); so the idea of "many" is the creation of the mind.

Differentiae become qualities when they are separate but joined in one object. We cannot say positively what differentiation is. All that we see and feel about things is pure and simple existence, *"isness"*. All else is in us. Being is the only positive proof we have of anything. All differentiation is really "secondary reality", as the snake in the rope, because the serpent, too, had a certain reality, in that *something* was seen although misapprehended. When the knowledge of the rope becomes negative, the knowledge of the snake becomes positive, and vice versa; but the fact that you see only one does not prove that the other is non-existent. The idea of the world is an obstruction covering the idea of God and is to be removed, but it does have an existence.

Shankara says again, perception is the last proof of existence. It is self-effulgent and self-conscious, because to go beyond the senses we should still need perception. Perception is independent of the senses, of all instruments, unconditioned. There can be no perception without consciousness; perception has self-luminosity, which in a lesser degree is called consciousness. Not one act of perception can be unconscious; in fact, consciousness is the nature of perception. Existence and perception are one thing, not two things joined together. That which is infinite; so, as perception is the last it is eternal. It is always subjective; is its own perceiver. Perception is not: perception brings mind. It is absolute, the only knower, so perception is really the Atman. Perception itself perceives, but the Atman cannot be a knower, because a "knower" becomes such by the action of knowledge; but, Shankara says, "This Atman is not I", because the consciousness "I am" (Aham) is not in the Atman. We are but the reflections of that Atman; and Atman and Brahman are one.

When you talk and think of the Absolute, you have to do it in the relative; so all these logical arguments apply. In Yoga, perception and realisation are one. Vishishtâdvaita, of which Ramanuja is the exponent, is seeing partial unity and is a step toward Advaita. Vishishta means differentiation. Prakriti is the nature of the world, and change comes upon it. Changeful thoughts expressed in changeful words can never prove the Absolute. You reach only something that is minus certain qualities, not Brahman Itself; only a verbal unification, the highest abstraction, but not the nonexistence of the relative.

Thursday, July 18, 1895.

(RECORDED BY MISS S. E. WALDO, A DISCIPLE)

(*The lesson today was mainly Shankara's argument against the conclusion of the Sânkhya philosophy.*)

The Sankhyas say that consciousness is a compound, and beyond that, the last analysis gives us the Purusha, Witness, but that there are many Purushas — each of us is one. Advaita, on the contrary, affirms that Purushas can be only One, that Purusha cannot be conscious, unconscious, or have any qualification, for either these qualities would bind, or they would eventually cease; so the One must be without any qualities, even knowledge, and It cannot be the cause of the universe or of anything. "In the beginning, existence only, One without a second", says the Vedas.

* * *

The presence of Sattva with knowledge does not prove that Sattva is the cause of knowledge; on the contrary, Sattva calls out what was already existing in man, as the fire heats an iron ball placed near it by arousing the heat latent in it, not by entering into the ball.

Shankara says, knowledge is not a bondage, because it is the nature of God. The world ever is, whether manifested or unmanifested; so an eternal object exists.

Jnâna-bala-kriyâ (knowledge, power, activity) is God. Nor does He need form, because the finite only needs form to interpose as an obstruction to catch and hold infinite knowledge; but God really needs no such help. There is no "moving soul", there is only one Atman. Jiva (individual soul) is the conscious ruler of this body, in whom the five life principles come into unity, and yet that very Jiva is the Atman, because all is Atman. What you think about it is your delusion and not in the Jiva. You are God, and whatever else you may think is wrong. You must worship the Self in Krishna, not Krishna as Krishna. Only by worshipping the Self can freedom be won. Even personal God is but the Self objectified. "Intense search after my own reality is Bhakti", says Shankara.

All the means we take to reach God are true; it is only like trying to find the pole-star by locating it through the stars that are around it.

* * *

The Bhagavad-Gita is the best authority on Vedanta.

Friday, July 19, 1895.

(RECORDED BY MISS S. E. WALDO, A DISCIPLE)

So long as I say "you", I have the right to speak of God protecting us. When I see another, I must take all the consequences and put in the third, the ideal, which stands between us; that is the apex of the triangle. The vapour becomes snow, then water, then Ganga; but when it is vapour, there is no Ganga, and when it is water, we think of no vapour in it. The idea of creation or change is inseparably connected with will. So long as we perceive this world in motion, we have to conceive will behind it. Physics proves the utter delusion of the senses; nothing really is as ever see, hear, feel, smell, taste it. Certain vibrations producing certain results affect our senses; we know only relative truth.

The Sanskrit word for truth is "isness" (Sat). From our present standpoint, this world appears to us as will and consciousness. Personal God is as much an entity for Himself as we are for ourselves, and no more. God can also be seen as a form, just as we are seen. As men, we must have a God; as God, we need none. This is why Shri Ramakrishna constantly saw the Divine Mother ever present with him, more real than any other thing around him; but in Samâdhi all went but the Self. Personal God comes nearer and nearer until He melts away, and there is no more Personal God and no more "I", all is merged in Self.

Consciousness is a bondage. The argument from design claims that intelligence precedes form; but if intelligence is the cause of anything, it itself is in its turn an effect. It is Maya. God creates us, and we create God, and this is Maya. The circle is unbroken; mind creates body, and body creates mind; the egg brings the chicken, the chicken the egg; the tree the seed, the seed the tree. The world is neither entirely differentiated nor yet entirely homogeneous. Man is free and must rise above both sides. Both are right in their place; but to reach truth, "isness", we must transcend all that we now know of existence, will, consciousness, doing, going, knowing. There is no real individuality of the Jiva (separate soul); eventually it, as a compound, will go to pieces. Only that which is beyond further analysis is "simple", and that alone is truth, freedom, immortality, bliss. All struggles for the preservation of this illusive individuality are really vices. All struggles to lose this individuality are virtues. Everything in the universe is trying to break down this individuality, either consciously or unconsciously. All morality is based upon the destruction of separateness or false individuality, because that is the cause of all sin. Morality exists first; later, religion codifies it. Customs come first, and then mythology follows to explain them. While things are happening, they come by a higher law than reasoning; that arises later in the attempt to understand them. Reasoning is not the motive power, it is "chewing the cud" afterwards. Reason is the historian of the actions of the human beings.

* * *

Buddha was a great Vedantist (for Buddhism was really only an offshoot of Vedanta), and Shankara is often called a "hidden Buddhist". Buddha made the analysis, Shankara made the synthesis out of it. Buddha never bowed down to anything — neither Veda, nor caste, nor priest, nor custom. He fearlessly reasoned so far as reason could take him. Such a fearless search for truth and such love for every living thing the world has never seen. Buddha was the Washington of the religious world; he conquered a throne only to give it to the world, as Washington did to the American people. He sought nothing for himself.

Saturday, July 20, 1895.

(RECORDED BY MISS S. E. WALDO, A DISCIPLE)

Perception is our only real knowledge or religion. Talking about it for ages will never make us know our soul. There is no difference between theories and atheism. In fact, the atheist is the truer man. Every step I take in the light is mine for ever. When you go to a country and see it, then it is yours. We have each to see for ourselves; teachers can only "bring the food", we must eat it to be nourished. Argument can never prove God save as a logical conclusion.

It is impossible to find God outside of ourselves. Our own souls contribute all the divinity that is outside of us. We are the greatest temple. The objectification is only a faint imitation of what we see within ourselves.

Concentration of the powers of the mind is our only instrument to help us see God. If you know one soul (your own), you know all souls, past, present, and to come. The will concentrates the mind, certain things excite and control this will, such as reason, love, devotion, breathing. The concentrated mind is a lamp that shows us every corner of the soul.

No one method can suit all. These different methods are not steps necessary to be taken one after another. Ceremonials are the lowest form; next God external, and after that God internal. In some cases gradation may be needed, but in many only one way is required. It would be the height of folly to say to everyone, "You must pass through Karma and Bhakti before you can reach Jnana."

Stick to your reason until you reach something higher; and you will know it to be higher, because it will not jar with reason. The stage beyond consciousness is inspiration (Samâdhi); but never mistake hysterical trances for the real thing. It is a terrible thing to claim this inspiration falsely, to mistake instinct for inspiration. There is no external test for inspiration, we know it ourselves; our guardian against mistake is negative — the voice of reason. All religion is going beyond reason, but reason is the only guide to get there. Instinct is like ice, reason is the water, and inspiration is the subtlest form or vapour; one follows the other. Everywhere is this eternal sequence — unconsciousness, consciousness, intelligence — matter, body, mind — and to us it seems as if the chain began with the particular link we first lay hold of. Arguments on both sides are of equal weight, and both are true. We must reach beyond both, to where there is neither the one nor the other. These successions are all Maya.

Religion is above reason, supernatural. Faith is not belief, it is the grasp on the Ultimate, an illumination. First hear, then reason and find out all that reason can give about the Atman; let the flood of reason flow over It, then take what remains. If nothing remains, thank God you have escaped a superstition. When you have determined that nothing *can* take away the Atman, that It stands every test, hold fast to this and teach it to all. Truth cannot be partial; it is for the good of all. Finally, in perfect rest and peace meditate upon It, concentrate your mind upon It, make yourself one with It. Then no speech is needed; silence will carry the truth. Do not spend your energy in talking, but meditate in silence; and do not let the rush of the outside world disturb you. When your mind is in the highest state, you are unconscious of it. Accumulate power in silence and become a dynamo of spirituality. What can a beggar give? Only a king can give, and he only when he wants nothing himself.

Hold your money merely as custodian for what is God's. Have no attachment for it. Let name and fame and money go; they are a terrible bondage. Feel the wonderful atmosphere of freedom. You are free, free, free! Oh, blessed am I! Freedom am I! I am the Infinite! In my soul I can find no beginning and no end. All is my Self. Say this unceasingly.

Sunday, July 21, 1895.

(RECORDED BY MISS S. E. WALDO, A DISCIPLE)

(Patanjali's Yoga Aphorisms)

Yoga is the science of restraining the Chitta (mind) from breaking into Vrittis (modifications). Mind is a mixture of sensation and feelings, or action and reaction; so it cannot be permanent. The mind has a fine body and through this it works on the gross body. Vedanta says that behind the mind is the real Self. It accepts the other two, but posits a third, the Eternal, the Ultimate, the last analysis, the unit, where there is no further compound. Birth is *re*-composition, death is *de*-composition, and the final analysis is where Atman is found; there being no further division possible, the perdurable is reached.

The whole ocean is present at the back of each wave, and all manifestations are waves, some very big, some small; yet all are the ocean in their essence, the whole ocean; but as waves each is a part. When the waves are stilled, then all is one; "a spectator without a spectacle", says Patanjali. When the mind is active, the Atman is mixed up with it. The repetition of old forms in quick succession is memory.

Be unattached. Knowledge is power, and getting one you get the other. By knowledge you can even banish the material world. When you can mentally get rid of one quality after another from any object until all are gone, you can at will make the object itself disappear from your consciousness.

Those who are ready, advance very quickly and can become Yogis in six months. The less developed may take several years; and anyone by faithful work and by giving up everything else and devoting himself solely to practice can reach the goal in twelve years. Bhakti will bring you there without any of these mental gymnastics, but it is a slower way.

Ishvara is the Atman as seen or grasped by mind. His highest name is Om; so repeat it, meditate on it, and think of all its wonderful nature and attributes. Repeating the Om continually is the only true worship. It is not a word, it is God Himself.

Religion gives you nothing new; it only takes off obstacles and lets you see your Self. Sickness is the first great obstacle; a healthy body is the best instrument. Melancholy is an almost insuperable barrier. If you have once known Brahman, never after can you be melancholy. Doubt, want of perseverance, mistaken ideas are other obstacles.

* * *

Prânas are subtle energies, sources of motion. There are ten in all, five inward and five outward. One great current flows upwards, and the other downwards. Prânâyâma is controlling the Pranas through breathing. Breath is the fuel, Prana is the steam, and the body is the engine. Pranayama has three parts, Puraka (in-breathing), Kumbhaka (holding the breath), Rechaka (out-breathing). . . .

The Guru is the conveyance in which the spiritual influence is brought to you. Anyone can teach, but the spirit must be passed on by the Guru to the Shishya (disciple), and that will fructify. The relation between Shishyas is that of brotherhood, and this is actually accepted by law in India. The Guru passes the thought power, the Mantra, that he has received from those before him; and nothing can be done without a Guru. In fact, great danger ensues. Usually without a Guru, these Yoga practices lead to lust; but with one, this seldom happens. Each Ishta has a Mantra. The Ishta is the ideal peculiar to the particular worshipper; the Mantra is the external word to express it. Constant repetition of the word helps to fix the ideal firmly in the mind. This method of worship prevails among religious devotees all over India.

Tuesday, July 23, 1895.

(RECORDED BY MISS S. E. WALDO, A DISCIPLE)

(*Bhagavad-Gita, Karma-Yoga*)

To attain liberation through work, join yourself to work but without desire, looking for no result. Such work leads to knowledge, which in turn brings emancipation. To give up work before you *know*, leads to misery. Work done for the Self gives no bondage. Neither desire pleasure nor fear pain from work. It is the mind and body that work, not I. Tell yourself this unceasingly and realise it. Try not to know that you work.

Do all as a sacrifice or offering to the Lord. Be in the world, but not of it, like the lotus leaf whose roots are in the mud but which remains always pure. Let your love go to all, whatever they do to you. A blind man cannot see colour, so how can we see evil unless it is in us? We compare what we see outside with what we find in ourselves and pronounce judgment accordingly. If we are pure, we cannot see impurity. It may exist, but not for us. See only God in every man, woman and child; see it by the *antarjyotis*, "inner light", and seeing that, we can see naught else. Do not want this world, because what you desire you get. Seek the Lord and the Lord only. The more power there is, the more bondage, the more fear. How much more afraid and miserable are we than the ant! Get out of it all and come to the Lord. Seek the science of the maker and not that of the made.

"I am the doer and the deed." "He who can stem the tide of lust and anger is a great Yogi."

"Only by practice and non-attachment can we conquer mind." . . .

Our Hindu ancestors sat down and thought on God and morality, and so have we brains to use for the same ends; but in the rush of trying to get gain, we are likely to lose them again.

* * *

The body has in itself a certain power of curing itself and many things can rouse this curative power into action, such as mental conditions, or medicine, or exercise, etc. As long as we are disturbed by physical conditions, so long we need the help of physical agencies. Not until we have got rid of bondage to the nerves, can we disregard them.

There is the unconscious mind, but it is below consciousness, which is just one part of the human organism. Philosophy is guess-work about the mind. Religion is based upon sense contact, upon seeing, the only basis of knowledge. What comes in contact with the superconscious mind is fact. Âptas are those who have "sensed" religion. The proof is that if you follow their method, you too will see. Each science requires its own particular method and instruments. An astronomer cannot show you the rings of Saturn by the aid of all the pots and pans in the kitchen. He needs a telescope. So, to see the great facts of religion, the methods of those who have already seen must be followed. The greater the science the more varied the means of studying it. Before we came into the world, God provided the means to get out; so all we have to do is to find the means. But do not fight over methods. Look only for realisation and choose the best method you can find to suit you. Eat the mangoes and let the rest quarrel over the basket. See Christ, then you will be a Christian. All else is talk; the less talking the better.

The message makes the messenger. The Lord makes the temple; not vice versa.

Learn until "the glory of the Lord shines through your face", as it shone through the face of Shvetaketu.

Guess against guess makes fight; but talk of what you have been, and no human heart can resist it. Paul was converted against his will by realisation.

Tuesday AFTERNOON. (*After dinner there was a short conversation in the course of which the Swami said:*)

Delusion creates delusion. Delusion creates itself and destroys itself, such is Maya. All knowledge (so-called), being based on Maya, is a vicious circle, and in time that very knowledge destroys itself. "Let go the rope", delusion cannot touch the Atman. When we lay hold of the rope — identify ourselves with Maya — she has power over us. Let go of it, be the Witness only, then you can admire the picture of the universe undisturbed.

Wednesday, July 24, 1895.

The powers acquired by the practice of Yoga are not obstacles for the Yogi who is perfect, but are apt to be so for the beginner, through the wonder and pleasure excited by their exercise. Siddhis are the powers which mark success in the practice; and they may be produced by various means, such as the repetition of a Mantra, by Yoga practice, meditation, fasting, or even by the use of herbs and drugs. The Yogi, who has conquered all interest in the powers acquired and who renounces all virtue arising from his actions, comes into the "cloud of virtue" (name of one of the states of Samadhi) and radiates holiness as a cloud rains water.

Meditation is on a series of objects, concentration is on one object.

Mind is cognised by the Atman, but it is not self-illuminated. The Atman cannot be the cause of anything. How can it be? How can the Purusha join itself to Prakriti (nature)? It does not; it is only illusively thought to do so. . . .

Learn to help without pitying or feeling that there is any misery. Learn to be the same to enemy and to friend; then when you can do that and no longer have any desire, the goal is attained.

Cut down the banyan tree of desire with the axe of non-attachment, and it will vanish utterly. It is all illusion. "He from whom blight and delusion have fallen, he who has conquered the evils of association, he alone is *âzâd* (free)."

To love anyone personally is bondage. Love all alike, then all desires fall off.

Time, the "eater of everything", comes, and all has to go. Why try to improve the earth, to paint the butterfly? It all has to go at last. Do not be mere white mice in a treadmill, working always and never accomplishing anything. Every desire is fraught with evil, whether the desire itself be good or evil. It is like a dog jumping for a piece of meat which is ever receding from his reach, and dying a dog's death at last. Do not be like that. Cut off all desire.

* * *

Paramâtman as ruling Maya is Ishvara; Paramâtman as under Maya is Jivâtman. Maya is the sum total of manifestation and will utterly vanish.

Tree-nature is Maya, it is really God-nature which we see under the veil of Maya. The "why" of anything is in Maya. To ask why Maya came is a useless question, because the answer can never be given in Maya, and beyond Maya who will ask it? Evil creates "why", not "why" the evil, and it is evil that asks "why". Illusion destroys illusion. Reason itself, being based upon contradiction, is a circle and has to kill itself. Sense-perception is an inference, and yet all inference comes from perception.

Ignorance reflecting the light of God is seen; but by itself it is zero. The cloud would not appear except as the sunlight falls on it.

There were four travellers who came to a high wall. The first one climbed with difficulty to the top and without looking back, jumped over. The second clambered up the wall, looked over, and with a shout of delight disappeared. The third in his turn climbed to the top, looked where his companions had gone, laughed with joy, and followed them. But the fourth one came back to tell what had happened to his fellow-travellers. The sign to us that there is something beyond is the laugh that rings back from those great ones who have plunged from Maya's wall.

* * *

Separating ourselves from the Absolute and attributing certain qualities to It give us Ishvara. It is the Reality of the universe as seen through our mind. Personal devil is the misery of the world seen through the minds of the superstitious.

Thursday, July 25, 1895.

(RECORDED BY MISS S. E. WALDO, A DISCIPLE)

(Patanjali's Yoga Aphorisms)

"Things may be done, caused to be done, or approved of", and the effect upon us is nearly equal.

Complete continence gives great intellectual and spiritual power. The Brahmachârin must be sexually pure in thought, word, and deed. Lose regard for the body; get rid of the consciousness of it so far as possible.

Âsana (posture) must be steady and pleasant; and constant practice, identifying the mind with the Infinite, will bring this about.

Continual attention to one object is contemplation.

When a stone is thrown into still water, many circles are made, each distinct but all interacting; so with our minds; only in us the action is unconscious, while with the Yogi it is conscious. We are spiders in a web, and Yoga practice will enable us like the spider to pass along any strand of the web we please. Non-Yogis are bound to the particular spot where they are.

* * *

To injure another creates bondage and hides the truth. Negative virtues are not enough; we have to conquer Maya, and then she will follow us. We only deserve things when they cease to bind us. When the bondage ceases, really and truly, all things come to us. Only those who want nothing are masters of nature.

Take refuge in some soul who has already broken his bondage, and in time he will free you through his mercy. Higher still is to take refuge in the Lord (Ishvara), but it is the most difficult; only once in a century can one be found who has really done it. Feel nothing, know nothing, do nothing, have nothing, give up all to God, and say utterly, "Thy will be done". We only dream this bondage. Wake up and let it go. Take refuge in God, only so can we cross the desert of Maya. "Let go thy hold, Sannyasin bold, say, Om tat sat, Om!"

It is our privilege to be allowed to be charitable, for only so can we grow. The poor man suffers that we may be helped; let the giver kneel down and give thanks, let the receiver stand up and permit. See the Lord back of every being and give to Him. When we cease to see evil, the world must end for us, since to rid us of that mistake is its only object. To think there is any imperfection creates it. Thoughts of strength and perfection alone can cure it. Do what good you can, some evil will inhere in it; but do all without regard to personal result, give up all results to the Lord, then neither good nor evil will affect you.

Doing work is not religion, but work done rightly leads to freedom. In reality all pity is darkness, because whom to pity? Can you pity God? And is there anything else? Thank God for giving you this world as a moral gymnasium to help your development, but never imagine you can help the world. Be grateful to him who curses you, for he gives you a mirror to show what cursing is, also a chance to practise self-restraint; so bless him and be glad. Without exercise, power cannot come out; without the mirror, we cannot see ourselves.

Unchaste imagination is as bad as unchaste action. Controlled desire leads to the highest result. Transform the sexual energy into spiritual energy, but do not emasculate, because that is throwing away the power. The stronger this force, the more can be done with it. Only a powerful current of water can do hydraulic mining.

What we need today is to know there is a God and that we can see and feel Him here and now. A Chicago professor says, "Take care of this world, God will take care of the next." What nonsense! If we can take care of this world, what need of a gratuitous Lord to take care of the other!

Friday, July 26, 1895.

(RECORDED BY MISS S. E. WALDO, A DISCIPLE)

(*Brihadâranyakopanishad.*)

Love all things only through and for the Self. Yâjnavalkya said to Maitreyi, his wife, "Through the Atman we know all things." The Atman can never be the object of knowledge, nor can the Knower be known. He who knows he is the Atman, he is law unto himself. He knows he is the universe and its creator. . . .

Perpetuating old myths in the form of allegories and giving them undue importance fosters superstition and is really weakness. Truth must have no compromise. Teach truth and make no apology for any superstition; neither drag truth to the level of the listener.

Saturday, July 27, 1895.

(RECORDED BY MISS S. E. WALDO, A DISCIPLE)

(*Kathopanishad*)

Learn not the truth of the Self save from one who has realised it; in all others it is mere talk. Realisation is beyond virtue and vice, beyond future and past; beyond all the pairs of opposites. "The stainless one sees the Self, and an eternal calm comes in the Soul." Talking, arguing, and reading books, the highest flights of the intellect, the Vedas themselves, all these cannot give knowledge of the Self.

In us are two — The God-soul and the man-soul. The sages know that the latter is but the shadow, that the former is the only real Sun.

Unless we join the mind with the senses, we get no report from eyes, nose, ears, etc. The external organs are used by the power of the mind. Do not let the senses go outside, and then you can get rid of body and the external world.

This very "x" which we see here as an external world, the departed see as heaven or hell according to their own mental states. Here and hereafter are two dreams, the latter modelled on the former; get rid of both, all is omnipresent, all is now. Nature, body, and mind go to death, not we; we never go nor come. The man Swami Vivekananda is in nature, is born, and dies; but the self which we see as Swami Vivekananda is never born and never dies. It is the eternal and unchangeable Reality.

The power of the mind is the same whether we divide it into five senses or whether we see only one. A blind man says, "Everything has a distinct echo, so I clap my hands and get that echo, and then I can tell everything that is around me." So in a fog the blind man can safely lead the seeing man. Fog or darkness makes no difference to him.

Control the mind, cut off the senses, then you are a Yogi; after that, all the rest will come. Refuse to hear, to see, to smell, to taste; take away the mental power from the external organs. You continually do it unconsciously as when your mind is absorbed; so you can learn to do it consciously. The mind can put the senses where it pleases. Get rid of the fundamental superstition that we are obliged to act through the body. We are not. Go into your own room and get the Upanishads out of your own Self. You are the greatest book that ever was or ever will be, the infinite depository of all that is. Until the inner teacher opens, all outside teaching is in vain. It must lead to the opening of the book of the heart to have any value.

The will is the "still small voice", the real Ruler who says "do" and "do not". It has done all that binds us. The ignorant will leads to bondage, the knowing will can free us. The will can be made strong in thousands of ways; every way is a kind of Yoga, but the systematised Yoga accomplishes the work more quickly. Bhakti, Karma, Raja, and Jnana-Yoga get over the ground more effectively. Put on all powers, philosophy, work, prayer, meditation — crowd all sail, put on all head of steam — reach the goal. The sooner, the better. . . .

Baptism is external purification symbolising the internal. It is of Buddhist origin.

The Eucharist is a survival of a very ancient custom of savage tribes. They sometimes killed their great chiefs and ate their flesh in order to obtain in themselves the qualities that made their leaders great. They believed that in such a way the characteristics that made the chief brave and wise would become theirs and make the whole tribe brave and wise, instead of only one man. Human sacrifice was also a Jewish idea and one that clung to them despite many chastisements from Jehovah. Jesus was gentle and loving, but to fit him into Jewish beliefs, the idea of human sacrifice, in the form of atonement or as a human scapegoat, had to come in. This cruel idea made Christianity depart from the teachings of Jesus himself and develop a spirit of persecution and bloodshed. . . .

Say, "it is my nature", never say, "It is my duty" — to do anything whatever.

"Truth alone triumphs, not untruth." Stand upon Truth, and you have got God.

* * *

From the earliest times in India the Brahmin caste have held themselves beyond all law; they claim to be gods. They are poor, but their weakness is that they seek power. Here are about sixty millions of people who are good and moral and hold no property, and they are what they are because from their birth they are taught that they are above law, above punishment. They feel themselves to be "twice-born", to be sons of God.

Sunday, July 28, 1895.

(RECORDED BY MISS S. E. WALDO, A DISCIPLE)

(Avadhuta Gita or "Song of the Purified" by Dattâtreya
(Dattatreya, the son of Atri and Anasuyâ, was an
incarnation of Brahmâ, Vishnu and Shiva.))

"All knowledge depends upon calmness of mind."

"He who has filled the universe, He who is Self in self, how shall I salute Him!"

To know the Atman as my nature is both knowledge and realisation. "I am He, there is not the least doubt of it."

"No thought, no word, no deed, creates a bondage for me. I am beyond the senses, I am knowledge and bliss."

There is neither existence nor non-existence, all is Atman. Shake off all ideas of relativity; shake off all superstitions; let caste and birth and Devas and all else vanish. Why talk of being and becoming? Give up talking of dualism and Advaitism! When were you two, that you talk of two or one? The universe is this Holy One and He alone. Talk not of Yoga to make you pure; you are pure by your very nature. None can teach you.

Men like him who wrote this song are what keep religion alive. They have actually realised; they care for nothing, feel nothing done to the body, care not for heat and cold or danger or anything. They sit still and enjoy the bliss of Atman, while red-hot coals burn their body, and they feel them not.

"When the threefold bondage of knower, knowledge, and known ceases, there is the Atman."

"Where the delusion of bondage and freedom ceases, there the Atman is."

"What if you have controlled the mind, what if you have not? What if you have money, what if you have not? You are the Atman ever pure. Say, 'I am the Atman. No bondage ever came near me. I am the changeless sky; clouds of belief may pass over me, but they do not touch me.'"

"Burn virtue, burn vice. Freedom is baby talk. I am that immortal Knowledge. I am that purity."

"No one was ever bound, none was ever free. There is none but me. I am the Infinite, the Ever-free. Talk not to me! What can change me, the essence of knowledge! Who can teach, who can be taught?"

Throw argument, throw philosophy into the ditch.

"Only a slave sees slaves, the deluded delusion, the impure impurity."

Place, time causation are all delusions. It is your disease that you think you are bound and will be free. You are the Unchangeable. Talk not. Sit down and let all things melt away, they are but dreams. There is no differentiation, no distinction, it is all superstition; therefore be silent and know what you are.

"I am the essence of bliss." Follow no ideal, you are all there is. Fear naught, you are the essence of existence. Be at peace. Do not disturb yourself. You never were in bondage, you never were virtuous or sinful. Get rid of all these delusions and be at peace. Whom to worship? Who worships? All is the Atman. To speak, to think is superstition. Repeat over and over, "I am Atman", "I am Atman". Let everything else go.

Monday, July 29, 1895.

(RECORDED BY MISS S. E. WALDO, A DISCIPLE)

We sometimes indicate a thing by describing its surroundings. When we say "Sachchidananda" (Existence-Knowledge-Bliss), we are merely indicating the shores of an indescribable Beyond. Not even can we say "is" about it, for that too is relative. Any imagination, any concept is in vain. Neti, neti ("Not this, not this") is all that can be said, for even to think is to limit and so to lose.

The senses cheat you day and night. Vedanta found that out ages ago; modern science is just discovering the same fact. A picture has only length and breadth, and the painter copies nature in her cheating by artificially giving the appearance of depth. No two people see the same world. The highest knowledge will show you that there is no motion, no change in anything; that the very idea of it is all Maya. Study nature as a whole, that is, study motion. Mind and body are not our real self; both belong to nature, but eventually we can know the *ding an sich*. Then mind and body being transcended, all that they conceive goes. When you cease utterly to know and see the world, then you realise Atman. The superseding of relative knowledge is what we want. There is no infinite mind or infinite knowledge, because both mind and knowledge are limited. We are now seeing through a veil; then we reach the "x", which is the Reality of all our knowing.

If we look at a picture through a pin-hole in a cardboard, we get an utterly mistaken notion; yet what we see is really the picture. As we enlarge the hole, we get a clearer and clearer idea. Out of the reality we manufacture the different views in conformity with our mistaken perceptions of name and form. When we throw away the cardboard, we see the same picture, but we see it as it is. We put in all the attributes, all the errors; the picture itself is unaltered thereby. That is because Atman is the reality of all; all we see is Atman, but not as we see it, as name and form; they are all in our veil, in Maya.

They are like spots in the object-glass of a telescope, yet it is the light of the sun that shows us the spots; we could not even see the illusion save for the background of reality which is Brahman. Swami Vivekananda is just the speck on the object-glass; I am Atman, real, unchangeable, and that reality alone enables me to see Swami Vivekananda. Atman is the essence of every hallucination; but the sun is never identified with the spots on the glass, it only shows them to us. Our actions, as they are evil or good, increase or decrease the "spots"; but they never affect the God within us. Perfectly cleanse the mind of spots and instantly we see, "I and my father are one".

We first perceive, then reason later. We must have this perception as a fact, and it is called religion, realisation. No matter if one never heard of creed or prophet or book. Let him get this realisation, and he needs no more. Cleanse the mind, this is all of religion; and until we ourselves clear off the spots, we cannot see the Reality as it is. The baby sees no sun; he has not yet the measure of it in himself. Get rid of the defects within yourself, and you will not be able to see any without. A baby sees robbery done, and it means nothing to him. Once you find the hidden object in a puzzle picture, you see it ever more; so when once you are free and stainless, you see only freedom and purity in the world around. That moment all the knots of the heart are cut asunder, all crooked places are made straight, and this world vanishes as a dream. And when we awake, we wonder how we ever came to dream such trash!

"Getting whom, misery mountain high has no power to move the soul."

With the axe of knowledge cut the wheels asunder, and the Atman stands free, even though the old momentum carries on the wheel of mind and body. The wheel can now only go straight, can only do good. If that body does anything bad, know that the man is not Jivanmukta; he lies if he makes that claim. But it is only when the wheels have got a good straight motion (from cleansing the mind) that the axe can be applied. All purifying action deals conscious or unconscious blows on delusion. To call another a sinner is the worst thing you can do. Good action done ignorantly produces the same result and helps to break the bondage.

To identify the sun with the spots on the object-glass is the fundamental error. Know the sun, the "I", to be ever unaffected by anything, and devote yourself to cleansing the spots. Man is the greatest being that ever can be. The highest worship there is, is to worship man as Krishna, Buddha, Christ. What you want, you create. Get rid of desire. . . .

The angels and the departed are all here, seeing this world as heaven. The same "x" is seen by all according to their mental attitude. The best vision to be had of the "x" is here on this earth. Never want to go to heaven, that is the worst delusion. Even here, too much wealth and grinding poverty are both bondages and hold us back from religion. Three great gifts we have: first, a human body. (The human mind is the nearest reflection of God, we are "His own image".) Second, the desire to be free. Third, the help of a noble soul, who has crossed the ocean of delusion, as a teacher. When you have these three, bless the Lord; you are sure to be free.

What you only grasp intellectually may be overthrown by a new argument; but what you realise is yours for ever. Talking, talking religion is but little good. Put God behind everything — man, animal, food, work; make this a habit.

Ingersoll once said to me: "I believe in making the most out of this world, in squeezing the orange dry, because this world is all we are sure of." I replied: "I know a better way to squeeze the orange of this world than you do, and I get more out of it. I *know* I cannot die, so I am not in a hurry; I know there is no fear, so I enjoy the squeezing. I have no duty, no bondage of wife and children and property; I can love all men and women. Everyone is God to me. Think of the joy of loving man as God! Squeeze your orange this way and get ten thousandfold more out of it. Get every single drop."

That which seems to be the will is the Atman behind, it is really free.

Monday AFTERNOON.

Jesus was imperfect because he did not live up fully to his own ideal, and above all because he did not give woman a place equal to man. Women did everything for him, and yet he was so bound by the Jewish custom that not one was made an apostle. Still he was the greatest character next to Buddha, who in his turn was not fully perfect. Buddha, however, recognised woman's right to an equal place in religion, and his first and one of his greatest disciples was his own wife, who became the head of the whole Buddhistic movement among the women of India. But we ought not to criticise these great ones, we should only look upon them as far above ourselves. Nonetheless we must not pin our faith to any man, however great; we too must become Buddhas and Christs.

No man should be judged by his defects. The great virtues a man has are his especially, his errors are the common weaknesses of humanity and should never be counted in estimating his character.

* * *

Vira, the Sanskrit word for "heroic", is the origin of our word "virtue", because in ancient times the best fighter was regarded as the most virtuous man.

Tuesday, July 30, 1895.

(RECORDED BY MISS S. E. WALDO, A DISCIPLE)

Christs and Buddhas are simply occasions upon which to objectify our own inner powers. We really answer our own prayers.

It is blasphemy to think that if Jesus had never been born, humanity would not have been saved. It is horrible to forget thus the divinity in human nature, a divinity that must come out. Never forget the glory of human nature. We are the greatest God that ever was or ever will be. Christs and Buddhas are but waves on the boundless ocean which *I am*. Bow down to nothing but your own higher Self. Until you know that you are that very God of gods, there will never be any freedom for you.

All our past actions are really good, because they lead us to what we ultimately become. Of whom to beg? I am the real existence, and all else is a dream save as it is I. I am the whole ocean; do not call the little wave you have made "I"; know it for nothing but a wave. Satyakâma (lover of truth) heard the inner voice telling him, "You are the infinite, the universal is in you. Control yourself and listen to the voice of your true Self."

The great prophets who do the fighting have to be less perfect than those who live silent lives of holiness, thinking great thoughts and so helping the world. These men, passing out one after another, produce as final outcome the man of power who preaches.

* * *

Knowledge exists, man only discovers it. The Vedas are the eternal knowledge through which God created the world. They talk high philosophy — the highest — and make this tremendous claim. . . .

Tell the truth boldly, whether it hurts or not. Never pander to weakness. If truth is too much for intelligent people and sweeps them away, let them go; the sooner the better. Childish ideas are for babies and savages; and these are not all in the nursery and the forests, some of them have fallen into the pulpits.

It is bad to stay in the church after you are grown up spiritually. Come out and die in the open air of freedom.

All progression is in the relative world. The human form is the highest and man the greatest being, because here and now we can get rid of the relative world entirely, can actually attain freedom, and this is the goal. Not only we can, but some have reached perfection; so no matter what finer bodies come, they could only be on the relative plane and could do no more than we, for to attain freedom is all that can be done.

The angels never do wicked deeds, so they never get punished and never get saved. Blows are what awaken us and help to break the dream. They show us the insufficiency of this world and make us long to escape, to have freedom. . . .

A thing dimly perceived we call by one name; the same thing when fully perceived we call by another. The higher the moral nature, the higher the perception and the stronger the will.

Tuesday AFTERNOON.

The reason of the harmony between thought and matter is that they are two sides of one thing, call it "x", which divides itself into the internal and the external.

The English word "paradise" comes from the Sanskrit *para-desa*, which was taken over into the Persian language and means literally "the land beyond", or the other world. The old Aryans always believed in a soul, never that man was the body. Their heavens and hells were all temporary, because no effect can outlast its cause and no cause is eternal; therefore all effects must come to an end.

The whole of the Vedanta Philosophy is in this story: Two birds of golden plumage sat on the same tree. The one above, serene, majestic, immersed in his own glory; the one below restless and eating the fruits of the tree, now sweet, now bitter. Once he ate an exceptionally bitter fruit, then he paused and looked up at the majestic bird above; but he soon forgot about the other bird and went on eating the fruits of the tree as before. Again he ate a bitter fruit, and this time he hopped up a few boughs nearer to the bird at the top. This happened many times until at last the lower bird came to the place of the upper bird and lost himself. He found all at once that there had never been two birds, but that he was all the time that upper bird, serene, majestic, and immersed in his own glory.

Wednesday, July 31, 1895.

Luther drove a nail into religion when he took away renunciation and gave us morality instead. Atheists and materialists can have ethics, but only believers in the Lord can have religion.

The wicked pay the price of the great soul's holiness. Think of that when you see a wicked man. Just as the poor man's labour pays for the rich man's luxury, so is it in the spiritual world. The terrible degradation of the masses in India is the price nature pays for the production of great souls like Mirâ-bâi, Buddha, etc.

* * *

"I am the holiness of the holy" (Gita). I am the root, each uses it in his own way, but all is I. "I do everything, you are but the occasion."

Do not talk much, but feel the spirit within you; then you are a Jnani. This is knowledge, all else is ignorance. All that is to be known is Brahman. It is the all. . . .

Sattva binds through the search for happiness and knowledge, Rajas binds through desire, Tamas binds through wrong perception and laziness. Conquer the two lower by Sattva, and then give up all to the Lord and be free.

The Bhakti-Yogi realises Brahman very soon and goes beyond the three qualities. (Gita, Chapter XII.)

The will, the consciousness, the senses, desire, the passions, all these combined make what we call the "soul".

There is first, the apparent self (body); second, the mental self who mistakes the body for himself (the Absolute bound by Maya); third, the Atman, the ever pure, the ever free. Seen partially, It is nature; seen wholly, all nature goes, even the memory of it is lost. There is the changeable (mortal), the eternally changeable (nature), and the Unchangeable (Atman).

Be perfectly hopeless, that is the highest state. What is there to hope for? Burst asunder the bonds of hope, stand on your Self, be at rest, never mind what you do, give up all to God, but have no hypocrisy about it.

Svastha, the Sanskrit word for "standing on your own Self", is used colloquially in India to inquire, "Are you well, are you happy?" And when Hindus would express, "I saw a thing", they say, "I saw a word-meaning (Padârtha)." Even this universe is a "word-meaning".

* * *

A perfect man's body mechanically does right; it can do only good because it is fully purified. The past momentum that carries on the wheel of body is all good. All evil tendencies are burnt out.

* * *

"That day is indeed a bad day when we do not speak of the Lord, not a stormy day."

Only love for the Supreme Lord is true Bhakti. Love for any other being, however great, is not Bhakti. The "Supreme Lord" here means Ishvara, the concept of which transcends what you in the West mean by the personal God. "He from whom this universe proceeds, in whom it rests, and to whom it returns, He is Ishvara, the Eternal, the Pure, the All-Merciful, the Almighty, the Ever-Free, the All-Knowing, the Teacher of all teachers, the Lord who of His own nature is inexpressible Love."

Man does not manufacture God out of his own brain; but he can only see God in the light of his own capacity, and he attributes to Him the best of all he knows. Each attribute is the whole of God, and this signifying the whole by one quality is the metaphysical explanation of the personal God. Ishvara is without form yet has all forms, is without qualities yet has all qualities. As human beings, we have to see the trinity of existence — God, man, nature; and we cannot do otherwise.

But to the Bhakta all these philosophical distinctions are mere idle talk. He cares nothing for argument, he does not reason, he "senses", he perceives. He wants to love himself in pure love of God, and there have been Bhaktas who maintain that this is more to be desired than liberation, who say, "I do not want to *be* sugar. I want to taste sugar; I want to love and enjoy the Beloved."

In Bhakti-Yoga the first essential is to want God honestly and intensely. We want everything but God, because our ordinary desires are fulfilled by the external world. So long as our needs are confined within the limits of the physical universe, we do not feel any need for God; it is only when we have had hard blows in our lives and are disappointed with everything here that we feel the need for something higher; then we seek God.

Bhakti is not destructive; it teaches that all our faculties may become means to reach salvation. We must turn them all towards God and give to Him that love which is usually wasted on the fleeting objects of sense.

Bhakti differs from your Western idea of religion in that Bhakti admits no elements of fear, no Being to be appeased or propitiated. There are even Bhaktas who worship God as their own child, so that there may remain no feeling even of awe or reverence. There can be no fear in true love, and so long as there is the least fear, Bhakti cannot even begin. In Bhakti there is also no place for begging or bargaining with God. The idea of asking God for anything is sacrilege to a Bhakta. He will not pray for health or wealth or even to go to heaven.

One who wants to love God, to be a Bhakta, must make a bundle of all these desires and leave them outside the door and then enter. He who wants to enter the realms of light must make a bundle of all "shop-keeping" religion and cast it away before he can pass the gates. It is not that you do not get what you pray for; you get everything, but it is low, vulgar, a beggar's religion. "Fool indeed is he, who, living on the banks of the Ganga, digs a little well for water. Fool indeed is the man who, coming to a mine of diamonds, begins to search for glass beads." These prayers for health and wealth and material prosperity are not Bhakti. They are the lowest form of Karma. Bhakti is a higher thing. We are striving to come into the presence of the King of kings. We cannot get there in a beggar's dress. If we wanted to enter the presence of an emperor, would we be admitted in a beggar's rags? Certainly not. The lackey would drive us out of the gates. This is the Emperor of emperors and never can we come before Him in a beggar's garb. Shop-keepers never have admission there, buying and selling will not do there at all. You read in the Bible that Jesus drove the buyers and sellers out of the temple.

So it goes without saying that the first task in becoming a Bhakta is to give up all desires of heaven and so on. Such a heaven would be like this place, this earth, only a little better. The Christian idea of heaven is a place of intensified enjoyment. How can that be God? All this desire to go to heaven is a desire for enjoyment. This has to be given up. The love of the Bhakta must be absolutely pure and unselfish, seeking nothing for itself either here or hereafter.

"Giving up the desire of pleasure and pain, gain or loss, worship God day and night; not a moment is to be lost in vain."

"Giving up all other thoughts, the whole mind day and night worships God. Thus being worshipped day and night, He reveals Himself and makes His worshippers feel Him."

Thursday, August 1, 1895.

(RECORDED BY MISS S. E. WALDO, A DISCIPLE)

The real Guru is the one through whom we have our spiritual descent. He is the channel through which the spiritual current flows to us, the link which joins us to the whole spiritual world. Too much faith in personality has a tendency to produce weakness and idolatry, but intense love for the Guru makes rapid growth possible, he connects us with the internal Guru. Adore your Guru if there be real truth in him; that Guru-bhakti (devotion to the teacher) will quickly lead you to the highest.

Sri Ramakrishna's purity was that of a baby. He never touched money in his life, and lust was absolutely annihilated in him. Do not go to great religious teachers to learn physical science, their whole energy has gone to the spiritual. In Sri Ramakrishna Paramahamsa the man was all dead and only God remained; he actually could not see sin, he was literally "of purer eyes than to behold iniquity". The purity of these few Paramahamsa (Monks of the highest order) is all that holds the world together. If they should all die out and leave it, the world would go to pieces. They do good by simply being, and they know it not; they just are. . . .

Books suggest the inner light and the method of bringing that out, but we can only understand them when we have earned the knowledge ourselves. When the inner light has flashed for you, let the books go, and look only within. You have in you all and a thousand times more than is in all the books. Never lose faith in yourself, you can do anything in this universe. Never weaken, all power is yours.

If religion and life depend upon books or upon the existence of any prophet whatsoever, then perish all religion and books! Religion is in us. No books or teachers can do more than help us to find it, and even without them we can get all truth within. You have gratitude for books and teachers without bondage to them; and worship your Guru as God, but do not obey him blindly; love him all you will, but think for yourself. No blind belief can save you, work out your own salvation. Have only one idea of God — that He is an eternal help.

Freedom and highest love must go together, then neither can become a bondage. We can give nothing to God; He gives all to us. He is the Guru of Gurus. Then we find that He is the "Soul of our souls", our very Self. No wonder we love Him, He is the Soul of our souls; whom or what else can we love? We want to be the "steady flame, burning without heat and without smoke". To whom can you do good, when you see only God? You cannot do good to God! All doubt goes, all is, "sameness". If you do good at all, you do it to yourself; feel that the receiver is the higher one. You serve the other because you are lower than he, not because he is low and you are high. Give as the rose gives perfume, because it is its own nature, utterly unconscious of giving.

The great Hindu reformer, Raja Ram Mohan Roy, was a wonderful example of this unselfish work. He devoted his whole life to helping India. It was he who stopped the burning of widows. It is usually believed that this reform was due entirely to the English; but it was Raja Ram Mohan Roy who started the agitation against the custom and succeeded in obtaining the support of the Government in suppressing it. Until he began the movement, the English had done nothing. He also founded the important religious Society called the Brahmo-Samaj, and subscribed a hundred thousand dollars to found a university. He then stepped out and told them to go ahead without him. He cared nothing for fame or for results to himself.

Thursday AFTERNOON.

There are endless series of manifestations, like "merry-go-round", in which the souls ride, so to speak. The series are eternal; individual souls get out, but the events repeat themselves eternally; and that is how one's past and future can be read, because all is really present. When the soul is in a certain chain, it has to go through the experiences of that chain. From one series souls go to other series; from some series they escape for ever by realising that they are Brahman. By getting hold of one prominent event in a chain and holding on to it, the whole chain can be dragged in and read. This power is easily acquired, but it is of no real value; and to practise it takes just so much from our spiritual forces. Go not after these things, worship God.

Friday, August 2, 1895.

(RECORDED BY MISS S. E. WALDO, A DISCIPLE)

Nishthâ (devotion to one ideal) is the beginning of realisation. "Take the honey out of all flowers; sit and be friendly with all, pay reverence to all, say to all, 'Yes, brother, yes, brother', but keep firm in your own way." A higher stage is actually to take the position of the other. If I am all, why can I not really and actively sympathise with my brother and see with his eyes? While I am weak, I must stick to one course (Nishthâ), but when I am strong, I can feel with every other and perfectly sympathise with his ideas.

The old idea was: "Develop one idea at the expense of all the rest". The modern way is "harmonious development". A third way is to "develop the mind and control it", then put it where you will; the result will come quickly. This is developing yourself in the truest way. Learn concentration and use it in any direction. Thus you lose nothing. He who gets the whole must have the parts too. Dualism is included in Advaitism (monism).

"I first saw him and he saw me. There was a flash of eye from me to him and from him to me."

This went on until the two souls became so closely united that they actually became one. . . .

There are two kinds of Samadhi — I concentrate on myself, then I concentrate and there is a unity of subject and object.

You must be able to sympathise fully with each particular, then at once to jump back to the highest monism. After having perfected yourself, you limit yourself voluntarily. Take the whole power into each action. Be able to become a dualist for the time being and forget Advaita, yet be able to take it up again at will.

* * *

Cause and effect are all Maya, and we shall grow to understand that all we see is as disconnected as the child's fairy tales now seem to us. There is really no such thing as cause and effect and we shall come to know it. Then if you can, lower your intellect to let any allegory pass through your mind without questioning about connection. Develop love of imagery and beautiful poetry and then enjoy all mythologies as poetry. Come not to mythology with ideas of history and reasoning. Let it flow as a current through your mind, let it be whirled as a candle before your eyes, without asking who holds the candle, and you will get the circle; the residuum of truth will remain in your mind.

The writers of all mythologies wrote in symbols of what they saw and heard, they painted flowing pictures. Do not try to pick out the themes and so destroy the pictures; take them as they are and let them act on you. Judge them only by the effect and get the good out of them.

* * *

Your own will is all that answers prayer, only it appears under the guise of different religious conceptions to each mind. We may call it Buddha, Jesus, Krishna, Jehovah, Allah, Agni, but it is only the Self, the "I". . . .

Concepts grow, but there is no historical value in the allegories which present them. Moses' visions are more likely to be wrong than ours are, because we have more knowledge and are less likely to be deceived by illusions.

Books are useless to us until our own book opens; then all other books are good so far as they confirm our book. It is the strong that understand strength, it is the elephant that understands the lion, not the rat. How can we understand Jesus until we are his equals? It is all in the dream to feed five thousand with two loaves, or to feed two with five loaves; neither is real and neither affects the other. Only grandeur appreciates grandeur, only God realises God. The dream is only the dreamer, it has no other basis. It is not one thing and the dreamer another. The keynote running through the music is — "I am He, I am He", all other notes are but variations and do not affect the real theme. We are the living books and books are but the words we have spoken. Everything is the living God, the living Christ; see it as such. Read man, he is the living poem. We are the light that illumines all the Bibles and Christs and Buddhas that ever were. Without that, these would be dead to us, not living.

Stand on your own Self.

The dead body resents nothing; let us make our bodies dead and cease to identify ourselves with them.

Saturday, August 3, 1895.

Individuals who are to get freedom in this life have to live thousands of years in one lifetime. They have to be ahead of their times, but the masses can only crawl. Thus we have Christs and Buddhas. . . .

There was once a Hindu queen, who so much desired that all her children should attain freedom in this life that she herself took all the care of them; and as she rocked them to sleep, she sang always the one song to them — "Tat tvam asi, Tat tvam asi" ("That thou art, That thou art").

Three of them became Sannyasins, but the fourth was taken away to be brought up elsewhere to become a king. As he was leaving home, the mother gave him a piece of paper which he was to read when he grew to manhood. On that piece of paper was written, "God alone is true. All else is false. The soul never kills or is killed. Live alone or in the company of holy ones." When the young prince read this, he too at once renounced the world and became a Sannyasin.

Give up, renounce the world. Now we are like dogs strayed into a kitchen and eating a piece of meat, looking round in fear lest at any moment some one may come and drive them out. Instead of that, be a king and know you own the world. This never comes until you give it up and it ceases to bind. Give up mentally, if you do not physically. Give up from the heart of your hearts. Have Vairâgya (renunciation). This is the real sacrifice, and without it, it is impossible to attain spirituality. Do not desire, for what you desire you get, and with it comes terrible bondage. It is nothing but bringing "noses on us," as in the case of the man who had three boons to ask. We never get freedom until we are self-contained. "Self is the Saviour of self, none else."

Learn to feel yourself in other bodies, to know that we are all one. Throw all other nonsense to the winds. Spit out your actions, good or bad, and never think of them again. What is done is done. Throw off superstition. Have no weakness even in the face of death. Do not repent, do not brood over past deeds, and do not remember your good deeds; be *âzâd* (free). The weak, the fearful, the ignorant will never reach Atman. You cannot undo, the effect must come, face it, but be careful never to do the same thing again. Give up the burden of all deeds to the Lord; give all, both good and bad. Do not keep the good and give only the bad. God helps those who do *not* help themselves.

"Drinking the cup of desire, the world becomes mad." Day and night never come together, so desire and the Lord can never come together. Give up desire.

* * *

There is a vast difference between saying "food, food" and eating it, between saying "water, water" and drinking it. So by merely repeating the words "God, God" we cannot hope to attain realisation. We must strive and practise.

Only by the wave falling back into the sea can it become unlimited, never as a wave can it be so. Then after it has become the sea, it can become the wave again and as big a one as it pleases. Break the identification of yourself with the current and know that you are free.

True philosophy is the systematising of certain perceptions. Intellect ends where religion begins. Inspiration is much higher than reason, but it must not contradict it. Reason is the rough tool to do the hard work; inspiration is the bright light which shows us all truth. The will to do a thing is not necessarily inspiration. . . .

Progression in Maya is a circle that brings you back to the starting point; but you start ignorant and come to the end with all knowledge. Worship of God, worship of the holy ones, concentration and meditation, and unselfish work, these are the ways of breaking away from Maya's net; but we must first have the strong desire to get free. The flash of light that will illuminate the darkness for us is in us; it is the knowledge that is our nature — there is no "birthright", we were never born. All that we have to do is to drive away the clouds that cover it.

Give up all desire for enjoyment in earth or heaven. Control the organs of the senses and control the mind. Bear every misery without even knowing that you are miserable. Think of nothing but liberation. Have faith in Guru, in his teachings, and in the surety that you can get free. Say "Soham, Soham" whatever comes. Tell yourself this even in eating, walking, suffering; tell the mind this incessantly — that what we see never existed, that there is only "I". Flash — the dream will break! Think day and night, this universe is zero, only God is. Have intense desire to get free.

All relatives and friends are but "old dry wells"; we fall into them and get dreams of duty and bondage, and there is no end. Do not create illusion by *helping* anyone. It is like a banyan tree, that spreads on and on. If you are a dualist, you are a fool to try to help God. If you are a monist, you know that you are God; where find duty? You have no duty to husband, child, friend. Take things as they come, lie still, and when your body floats, go; rise with the rising tide, fall with falling tide. Let the body die; this idea of body is but a worn-out fable. "Be still and know that you are God."

The present only is existent. There is no past or future even in thought, because to think it, you have to make it the present. Give up everything, and let it float where it will. This world is all a delusion, do not let it fool you again. You have known it for what it is not, now know it for what it is. If the body is dragged anywhere, let it go; do not care where the body is. This tyrannical idea of duty is a terrible poison and is destroying the world.

Do not wait to have a harp and rest by degrees; why not take a harp and begin here? Why wait for heaven? Make it here. In heaven there is no marrying or giving in marriage; why not begin at once and have none here? The yellow robe of the Sannyasin is the sign of the free. Give up the beggar's dress of the world; wear the flag of freedom, the ochre robe.

Sunday, August 4, 1895.

(RECORDED BY MISS S. E. WALDO, A DISCIPLE)

"Whom the ignorant worship, Him I preach unto thee."

This one and only God is the "knownest" of the known. He is the one thing we see everywhere. All know their own Self, all know, "I am", even animals. All we know is the projection of the Self. Teach this to the children, they can grasp it. Every religion has worshipped the Self, even though unconsciously, because there is nothing else.

This indecent clinging to life as we know it here, is the source of all evil. It causes all this cheating and stealing. It makes money a god and all vices and fears ensue. Value nothing material and do not cling to it. If you cling to nothing, not even life, then there is no fear. "He goes from death to death who sees many in this world." There can be no physical death for us and no mental death, when we see that all is one. All bodies are mine; so even body is eternal, because the tree, the animal, the sun, the moon, the universe itself is my body; then how can it die? Every mind, every thought is mine, then how can death come? The Self is never born and never dies. When we realise this, all doubts vanish. "I am, I know, I love" — these can never be doubted. There is no hunger, for all that is eaten is eaten by me. If a hair falls out, we do not think we die; so if one body dies, it is but a hair falling. . . .

The superconscious is God, is beyond speech beyond thought, beyond consciousness. . . . There are three states, — brutality (Tamas), humanity (Rajas), and divinity (Sattva). Those attaining the highest state simply are. Duty dies there; they only love and as a magnet draw others to them. This is freedom. No more you do moral acts, but whatever you do is moral. The Brahmavit (knower of God) is higher than all gods. The angels came to worship Jesus when he had conquered delusion and had said, "Get thee behind me, Satan." None can help a Brahmavit, the universe itself bows down before him. His every desire is fulfilled, his spirit purifies others; therefore worship the Brahmavit if you wish to attain the highest. When we have the three great "gifts of God" — a human body, intense desire to be free, and the help of a great soul to show us the way — then liberation is certain for us. Mukti is ours.

* * *

Death of the body for ever is Nirvana. It is the negative side and says, "I am not this, nor this, nor this." Vedanta takes the further step and asserts the positive side — Mukti or freedom. "I am Existence absolute, Knowledge absolute, Bliss absolute, I am He", this is Vedanta, the cap-stone of the perfect arch.

The great majority of the adherents of Northern Buddhism believe in Mukti and are really Vedantists. Only the Ceylonese accept Nirvana as annihilation.

No belief or disbelief can kill the "I". That which comes with belief and goes with disbelief is only delusion. Nothing teaches the Atman. "I salute my own Self." "Self-illuminated, I salute myself, I am Brahman." The body is a dark room; when we enter it, it becomes illuminated, it becomes alive. Nothing can ever affect the illumination; it cannot be destroyed. It may be covered, but never destroyed.

* * *

At the present time God should be worshipped as "Mother", the Infinite Energy. This will lead to purity, and tremendous energy will come here in America. Here no temples weigh us down, no one suffers as they do in poorer countries. Woman has suffered for aeons, and that has given her infinite patience and infinite perseverance. She holds on to an idea. It is this which makes her the support of even superstitious religions and of the priests in every land, and it is this that will free her. We have to become Vedantists and live this grand thought; the masses must get it, and only in free America can this be done. In India these ideas were brought out by individuals like Buddha, Shankara, and others, but the masses did not retain them. The new cycle must see the masses living Vedanta, and this will have to come through women.

"Keep the beloved beautiful Mother in the heart of your hearts with all care."

"Throw out everything but the tongue, keep that to say, "Mother, Mother!"

"Let no evil counsellors enter; let you and me, my heart, alone see Mother."

"Thou art beyond all that lives!"

"My Moon of life, my Soul of soul!"

Sunday AFTERNOON.

Mind is an instrument in the hand of Atman, just as body is an instrument in the hand of mind. Matter is motion outside, mind is motion inside. All change begins and ends in time. If the Atman is unchangeable, It must be perfect; if perfect, It must be infinite; and if It be infinite, It must be only One; there cannot be two infinites. So the Atman, the Self, can be only One. Though It seems to be various, It is really only One. If a man were to go toward the sun, at every step he would see a different sun, and yet it would be the same sun after all.

Asti, "isness", is the basis of all unity; and just as soon as the basis is found, perfection ensues. If all colour could be resolved into one colour, painting would cease. The perfect oneness is rest; we refer all manifestations to one Being. Taoists, Confucianists, Buddhists, Hindus, Jews, Mohammedans, Christians, and Zoroastrians, all preached the golden rule and in almost the same words; but only the Hindus have given the rationale, because they saw the reason: Man must love others because those others are himself. There is but One.

Of all the great religious teachers the world has known, only Lao-tze, Buddha, and Jesus transcended the golden rule and said, "Do good to your enemies", "Love them that hate you."

Principles exist; we do not create them, we only discover them. . . . Religion consists solely in realisation. Doctrines are methods, not religion. All the different religions are but applications of the one religion adapted to suit the requirements of different nations. Theories only lead to fighting; thus the name of God that ought to bring peace has been the cause of half the bloodshed of the world. Go to the direct source. Ask God what He is. Unless He answers, He is not; but every religion teaches that He does answer.

Have something to say for yourself, else how can you have any idea of what others have said? Do not cling to old superstitions; be ever ready for new truths. "Fools are they who would drink brackish water from a well that their forefathers have digged and would not drink pure water from a well that others have digged." Until we realise God for ourselves, we can know nothing about Him. Each man is perfect by his nature; prophets have manifested this perfection, but it is potential in us. How can we understand that Moses saw God unless we too see Him? If God ever came to anyone, He will come to me. I will go to God direct; let Him talk to me. I cannot take belief as a basis; that is atheism and blasphemy. If God spake to a man in the deserts of Arabia two thousand years ago, He can also speak to me today, else how can I know that He has not died? Come to God any way you can; only come. But in coming do not push anyone down.

The knowing ones must have pity on the ignorant. One who knows is willing to give up his body even for an ant, because he knows that the body is nothing.

Monday, August 5, 1895.

The question is: Is it necessary to pass through all the lower stages to reach the highest, or can a plunge be taken at once? The modern American boy takes twenty-five years to attain that which his forefathers took hundreds of years to do. The present-day Hindu gets in twenty years to the height reached in eight thousand years by his ancestors. On the physical side, the embryo goes from the amoeba to man in the womb. These are the teachings of modern science. Vedanta goes further and tells us that we not only have to live the life of all past humanity, but also the future life of all humanity. The man who does the first is the educated man, the second is the Jivanmukta, for ever free (even while living).

Time is merely the measure of our thoughts, and thought being inconceivably swift, there is no limit to the speed with which we can live the life ahead. So it cannot be stated how long it would take to live all future life. It might be in a second, or it might take fifty lifetimes. It depends on the intensity of the desire. The teaching must therefore be modified according to the needs of the taught. The consuming fire is ready for all, even water and chunks of ice quickly consume. Fire a mass of bird-shot, one at least will strike; give a man a whole museum of truths, he will at once take what is suited to him. Past lives have moulded our tendencies; give to the taught in accordance with his tendency. Intellectual, mystical, devotional, practical — make one the basis, but teach the others with it. Intellect must be balanced with love, the mystical nature with reason, while practice must form part of every method. Take every one where he stands and push him forward. Religious teaching must always be constructive, not destructive.

Each tendency shows the life-work of the past, the line or radius along which that man must move. All radii lead to the centre. Never even attempt to disturb anyone's tendencies; to do that puts back both teacher and taught. When you teach Jnana, you must become a Jnani and stand mentally exactly where the taught stands. Similarly in every other Yoga. Develop every faculty as if it were the only one possessed, this is the true secret of so-called harmonious development. That is, get extensity with intensity, but not at its expense. We are infinite. There is no limitation in us, we can be as intense as the most devoted Mohammedan and as broad as the most roaring atheist.

The way to do this is not to put the mind on any one subject, but to develop and control the mind itself; then you can turn it on any side you choose. Thus you keep the intensity and extensity. Feel Jnana as if it were all there was, then do the same with Bhakti, with Raja (-Yoga), with Karma. Give up the waves and go to the ocean, then you can have the waves as you please. Control the "lake" of your own mind, else you cannot understand the lake of another's mind.

The true teacher is one who can throw his whole force into the tendency of the taught. Without real sympathy we can never teach well. Give up the notion that man is a responsible being, only the perfect man is responsible. The ignorant have drunk deep of the cup of delusion and are not sane. You, who *know*, must have infinite patience with these. Have nothing but love for them and find out the disease that has made them see the world in a wrong light, then help them to cure it and see aright. Remember always that only the free have free will; all the rest are in bondage and are not responsible for what they do. Will as will is bound. The water when melting on the top of the Himalayas is free, but becoming the river, it is bound by the banks; yet the original impetus carries it to the sea, and it regains its freedom. The first is the "fall of man", the second is the "resurrection". Not one atom can rest until it finds its freedom.

Some imaginations help to break the bondage of the rest. The whole universe is imagination, but one set of imaginations will cure another set. Those which tell us that there is sin and sorrow and death in the world are terrible; but the other set which says ever, "I am holy, there is God, there is no pain", these are good and help to break the bondage of the others. The highest imagination that can break all the links of the chain is that of Personal God.

"Om tat sat" is the only thing beyond Maya, but God exists eternally. As long as the Niagara Falls exist, the rainbow will exist; but the water continually flows away. The falls are the universe, and the rainbow is personal God; and both are eternal. While the universe exists, God must exist. God creates the universe, and the universe creates God; and both are eternal. Maya is neither existence nor non-existence. Both the Niagara Falls and the rainbow are eternally changeable. . . . Brahman seen through Maya. Persians and Christians split Maya into two and call the good half "God" and the bad half the "devil". Vedanta takes Maya as a whole and recognises a unity beyond it — Brahman. . . .

Mohammed found that Christianity was straying out from the Semitic fold and his teachings were to show what Christianity ought to be as a Semitic religion, that it should hold to one God. The Aryan idea that "I and my Father are one" disgusted and terrified him. In reality the conception of the Trinity was a great advance over the dualistic idea of Jehovah, who was for ever separate from man. The theory of incarnation is the first link in the chain of ideas leading to the recognition of the oneness of God and man. God appearing first in one human form, then re-appearing at different times in other human forms, is at last recognised as being in every human form, or in all men. Monistic is the highest stage, monotheistic is a lower stage. Imagination will lead you to the highest even more rapidly and easily than reasoning.

Let a few stand out and live for God alone and save religion for the world. Do not pretend to be like Janaka when you are only the "progenitor" of delusions. (The name Janaka means "progenitor" and belonged to a king who, although he still held his kingdom for the sake of his people, had given up everything mentally.) Be honest and say, "I see the ideal but I cannot yet approach it"; but do not pretend to give up when you do not. If you give up, stand fast. If a hundred fall in the fight, seize the flag and carry it on. God is true for all that, no matter who fails. Let him who falls hand on the flag to another to carry on; it can never fall.

When I am washed and clean, why shall impurity be added on to me? Seek first the kingdom of Heaven, and let everything else go. Do not want anything "added into you"; be only glad to get rid of it. Give up and know that success will follow, even if you never see it. Jesus left twelve fishermen, and yet those few blew up the Roman Empire.

Sacrifice on God's altar earth's purest and best. He who struggles is better than he who never attempts. Even to look on one who has given up has a purifying effect. Stand up for God; let the world go. Have no compromise. Give up the world, then alone you are loosened from the body. When it dies, you are *âzâd*, free. Be free. Death alone can never free us. Freedom must be attained by our own efforts during life; then, when the body falls, there will be no rebirth for the free.

Truth is to be judged by truth and by nothing else. Doing good is not the test of truth; the Sun needs no torch by which to see it. Even if truth destroys the whole universe, still it is truth; stand by it.

Practising the concrete forms of religion is easy and attracts the masses; but really there is nothing in the external.

"As the spider throws her web out of herself and draws it in, even so this universe is thrown out and drawn in by God."

Tuesday, August 6, 1895.

(R ECORDED BY M ISS S. E. W
ALDO , A DISCIPLE)

Without the "I" there can be no "you" outside. From this some philosophers came to the conclusion that the external world did not exist save in the subject; that the "you" existed only in the "I". Others have argued that the "I" can only be known through the "you" and with equal logic. These two views are partial truths, each wrong in part and each right in part. Thought is as much material and as much in nature as body is. Both matter and mind exist in a third, a unity which divides itself into the two. This unity is the Atman, the real Self.

There is being, "x", which is manifesting itself as both mind and matter. Its movements in the seen are along certain fixed lines called law. As a unity, it is free; as many, it is bound by law. Still, with all this bondage, an idea of freedom is ever present, and this is Nivritti, or the "dragging from attachment". The materialising forces which through desire lead us to take an active part in worldly affairs are called Pravritti.

That action is moral which frees us from the bondage of matter and vice versa. This world appears infinite, because everything is in a circle; it returns to whence it came. The circle meets, so there is no rest or peace here in any place. We must get out. Mukti is the one end to be attained. . . .

Evil changes in form but remains the same in quality. In ancient times force ruled, today it is cunning. Misery in India is not so bad as in America, because the poor man here sees the greater contrast to his own bad condition.

Good and evil are inextricably combined, and one cannot be had without the other. The sum total of energy in this universe is like a lake, every wave inevitably leads to a corresponding depression. The sum total is absolutely the same; so to make one man happy is to make another unhappy. External happiness is material and the supply is fixed; so that not one grain can be had by one person without taking from another. Only bliss beyond the material world can be had without loss to any. Material happiness is but a transformation of material sorrow.

Those who are born in the wave and kept in it do not see the depression and what is there. Never think, you can make the world better and happier.

The bullock in the oil-mill never reaches the wisp of hay tied in front of him, he only grinds out the oil. So we chase the will-o'-the-wisp of happiness that always eludes us, and we only grind nature's mill, then die, merely to begin again. If we could get rid of evil, we should never catch a glimpse of anything higher; we would be satisfied and never struggle to get free. When man finds that all search for happiness in matter is nonsense, then religion begins. All human knowledge is but a part of religion.

In the human body the balance between good and evil is so even that there is a chance for man to wish to free himself from both.

The free never became bound; to ask how he did, is an illogical question. Where no bondage is, there is no cause and effect. "I became a fox in a dream and a dog chased me." Now how can I ask why the dog chased me? The fox was a part of the dream, and the dog followed as a matter of course; but both belong to the dream and have no existence outside. Science and religion are both attempts to help us out of the bondage; only religion is the more ancient, and we have the superstition that it is the more holy. In a way it is, because it makes morality a vital point, and science does not.

"Blessed are the pure in heart, for they shall see God." This sentence alone would save mankind if all books and prophets were lost. This purity of heart will bring the vision of God. It is the theme of the whole music of this universe. In purity is no bondage. Remove the veils of ignorance by purity, then we manifest ourselves as we really are and know that we were never in bondage. The seeing of many is the great sin of all the world. See all as Self and love all; let all idea of separateness go. . . .

The diabolical man is a part of my body as a wound or a burn is. We have to nurse it and get it better; so continually nurse and help the diabolical man, until he "heals" and is once happy and healthy.

While we think on the relative plane, we have the right to believe that as bodies we can be hurt by relative things and equally that we can be helped by them. This idea of help, abstracted, is what we call God. The sum total of all ideas of help is God.

God is the abstract compound of all that is merciful and good and helpful; that should be the sole idea. As Atman, we have no body; so to say, "I am God, and poison does not hurt me", is an absurdity. While there is a body and we see it, we have not realised God. Can the little whirlpool remain after the river vanishes? Cry for help, and you will get it; and at last you will find that the one crying for help has vanished, and so has the Helper, and the play is over; only the Self remains.

This once done, come back and play as you will. This body can then do no evil, because it is not until the evil forces are all burned out that liberation comes. All dross has been burned out and there remains "flame without heat and without smoke".

The past momentum carries on the body, but it can only do good, because the bad was all gone before freedom came. The dying thief on the cross reaped the effects of his past actions. He had been a Yogi and had slipped; then he had to be born again; again he slipped and became a thief; but the past good he had done bore fruit, and he met Jesus in the moment when liberation could come, and one word made him free.

Buddha set his greatest enemy free, because he, by hating him (Buddha) so much, kept constantly thinking of him; that thought purified his mind, and he became ready for freedom. Therefore think of God all the time, and that will purify you. . . .

(*Thus ended the beautiful lessons of our beloved Guru. The following Monday he left Thousand Island Park and returned to New York.*)